U.S.-CHINA RELATIONS SINCE WORLD WAR II

8746
327.73°
H00

BY DOROTHY AND THOMAS HOOBLER

FRANKLIN WATTS
NEW YORK | LONDON | TORONTO | SYDNEY | 1981
AN IMPACT BOOK

Photographs courtesy of:

United Press International:
pp. 9, 32, 42, 72, 84, 87;

U.S. Army: p. 14.

Library of Congress Cataloging in Publication Data

Hoobler, Dorothy.
U.S.–China relations since World War II.

(An Impact book)
Bibliography: p.
Includes index.
SUMMARY: Discusses the United States' relationship
with the world's oldest civilization from 1784
when American traders set sail for China to the
opening of full relations following the Vietnam War.
1. United States—Foreign relations—China—
Juvenile literature. 2. China—Foreign relations
—United States—Juvenile literature.
[1. United States—Foreign relations—China.
2. China—Foreign relations—United States]
I. Hoobler, Thomas, joint author.
II. Title.
E183.8.C5H68   327.73051   80–25343
ISBN 0–531–04264–2

CONTENTS

ABOUT THE SPELLING
OF CHINESE PROPER NAMES
IN THIS BOOK

The Chinese language is written with pictographic characters that do not correspond to the twenty-six letters of the English language. Nor are the sounds made in spoken Chinese easily represented by English characters. The difficulty of representing Chinese proper names in English presents problems of standardization even today.

Around 1860, two British scholars, Sir Thomas Wade and Herbert A. Giles, devised the Wade-Giles system of representing Chinese proper names in English. Their system, with some modifications, remained in general use until 1979. At that time, the government of the People's Republic of China decreed that another system, called "Pinyin," meaning "transcription," be used by its foreign ministry and the official press agency. Major English-language newspapers, such as *The Washington Post* and *The New York Times,* now use the Pinyin system for printing Chinese names. (The Nationalist government on Taiwan, however, still uses the Wade-Giles system in communicating with foreigners.)

Because virtually all the books in our For Further Reading list use the modified Wade-Giles system for historical persons and place-names, we have used the more familiar Wade-Giles for Chinese individuals whose importance preceded the death of Mao Tse-tung. The names of Chinese officials who formed the post-Mao government are represented in this book according to the Pinyin system.

For the reader's convenience, a list follows comparing the Wade-Giles and Pinyin spellings of Chinse proper names used in this book.

Modified Wade-Giles	Pinyin	Modified Wade-Giles	Pinyin
PLACES		PEOPLE	
Canton	Guangzhou	Chai Tse-min	Chai Zemin
Chungking	Chongqing	Chiang Kai-shek	Jiang Jieshi
Dairen	Dalian	Chou En-lai	Zhou Enlai
Hunan	Hunan	Chu Teh	Zhu De
Kaifeng	Kaifeng	Hua Kuo-feng	Hua Guofeng
Kiangsi	Jiangxi	Huang Hua	Huang Hua
Manchuria	Dongbei	Lin Piao	Lin Biao
Matsu	Mazu	Liu Shao-chi	Liu Shaoqi
Nanchang	Nanchang	Mao Tse-tung	Mao Zedong
Nanking	Nanjing	Teng Hsiao-ping	Deng Xiaoping
Peking	Beijing		
Shanghai	Shanghai		
Shantung	Shandong		
Shensi	Shaanxi		
Sinkiang	Xinjiang		
Tibet	Xizang		
Tientsin	Tianjin		
Quemoy	Jinmen		
Wuhan	Wuhan		
Yangtze	Changjiang		
Yenan	Yanan		

U.S.–CHINA RELATIONS SINCE WORLD WAR II

INTRODUCTION

The United States' relationship with the world's oldest civilization—China—goes back to the earliest years of the American republic. Yet despite their long relationship, the two countries have seldom fully understood each other. Though both are large and populous, their differences are far greater.

China, with its vast population that some say reached one billion in 1980, still is in the throes of industrial revolution and struggles to balance the needs of a modern power against the necessity of wresting from the soil enough food for its people. Human labor is still cheaper in China than machinery, while the United States has one of the world's highest standards of living.

In the earliest stages of the China–U.S. relationship, China regarded itself as the center of the world—the "Middle Kingdom"—which deigned to trade with foreigners only by imperial consent. Contact with the rest of the world was a rude shock to China, which was humbled and nearly carved up among the Europeans, Americans, and Japanese.

America regarded China with an attitude of benevolent superiority, first thinking it could Christianize it, then believing it could guide China's destiny. It took many shocks and reverses for America to discover that it could not mold China in the American image. As late as 1940, an American senator could say, "With God's help, we'll lift Shanghai up and up, ever up, until it's just like Kansas City."

What has taken Americans so long to discover is that the Chinese want a China that is theirs alone. It has been a bitter lesson, for Americans have a firm belief in their own goodness and for most of the twentieth century have wished to share their view of themselves with the rest of the world.

When China finally won control of its own destiny and embraced an ideology hostile to the United States, the two countries became estranged. The United States turned its back on the half-billion or more Chinese on the mainland and sought to keep them from participating in the affairs of the world.

An even more agonizing defeat, in Vietnam, brought America once again face-to-face with China. A new relationship was forged on the basis of mutual national interests, one in which both China and the United States seek to use the other as their chief card in world politics.

How well the people of the two countries understand each other will determine the course of this new relationship. This book aims to be a contribution toward that understanding, for only by comprehending the past can the future be determined.

CHINA AND THE UNITED STATES, 1784–1945

The relationship between the United States and China began in 1784, when the American trading ship *Empress of China* set sail from New York Harbor, bound for the Chinese port of Canton. American traders were lured by the prospect of "four hundred million" potential Chinese customers.

To the Chinese, the trade prospects offered by the Western nations were not so alluring. China had for centuries regarded itself as the center of the world and viewed all foreigners as barbarians. Foreign trade was confined to a limited area at the port of Canton, where Americans became known as "the new people" who had followed the Europeans already there.

THE OPIUM WARS

Chinese limitation on foreign trade was a source of contention that came to a head during the First Opium War of 1839–42. When Chinese officials seized a cargo of opium that the British used illegally as a trading lure, the British navy responded with warships. European military might humiliated the Chinese, who were forced to open more ports and areas to Western interests. On the heels of the British victory, the United States concluded the Treaty of Wanghia with the Chinese government in 1844. In the "most-favored-nation" clause of this treaty, China agreed to extend to the United States any trade concessions it might grant to any other nation in the future.

In addition to trade rights, the United States won the right to send missionaries to China and the right of "extraterritoriality," which meant that Americans could not be tried in Chinese courts for crimes committed on Chinese soil.

The presence of American missionaries in China served to increase Americans' belief that they could influence the destiny of China. Even though the missionaries were never able to convert as much as one percent of China's people, their observations on Chinese willingness to accept Western religions and Western ideas influenced opinion in the United States. Local church congregations raised funds for the missionary effort, feeling a sense of pride at helping to raise China from its "heathen" ways.

The first Chinese to come in large numbers to the United States arrived during the California gold rush of 1849. Chinese workers became an important source of labor in the building of the transcontinental railroad after the American Civil War, and after its completion were often found in mining towns throughout the West. Meeting with deep-seated racial prejudice, the Chinese were finally barred from immigration by the Chinese Exclusion Act of 1882. The law put the Chinese in a category with "imbeciles, paupers, and prostitutes."

Weakened by an ineffective government, China became a tempting prize for more powerful countries. At the end of the nineteenth century, Japan became as aggressive in its intentions toward China as the European countries. The Sino-Japanese War of 1894–95 resulted in China's ceding Korea, Formosa, and the Pescadores Islands to Japan. Japan also gained extraterritorial rights for Japanese in China, as well as the most-favored-nation treaty rights. In addition, Japan and Russia began to carve up "spheres of influence" in Manchuria, a resource-rich part of northern China.

THE "OPEN DOOR" POLICY

The United States viewed these developments with concern. It emerged as a world power in the 1890s, and its victory in the Spanish-American War brought it territory and influence in the Western Pacific. In 1898 the United States annexed Hawaii and the Philippines. Secretary of State John Hay felt that it was necessary to move to protect American trading rights in China. In 1899 he sent a series of notes to the countries holding spheres of influence in China, calling for them not to restrict Chinese trade with other nations.

In 1900 Hay sent a second series of notes, asking foreign powers to respect the territorial integrity of China. Hay's notes began the American policy of "the Open Door" toward China, which sought to keep China an open market by supporting Chinese territorial and administrative independence.

Foreign exploitation brought internal unrest to China. In 1900 a secret society known as the Boxers besieged the foreign diplomatic compound in the capital city of Peking. A multinational armed force, including U.S. Marines, fought its way into Peking and rescued the embassies. The foreign victors imposed a large indemnity on the Chinese and assumed control of Chinese tariffs on imports. In a goodwill gesture in 1908, the United States remitted its part of the indemnity and used it to enable Chinese students to study in the United States.

Inconsistencies in the American policy were noted by the Chinese. Although the United States was guaranteed access to trade in China, reciprocal rights for Chinese trade in the United States were not granted; the United States continued its policy of discrimination against the immigration of Chinese. In 1905 the Chinese boycotted American goods to show their disapproval of the American policies.

Since the signing of the Treaty of Wanghia and similar treaties with European nations that came collectively to be known as the "unequal treaties," the Chinese had felt humiliated by their imperial government's inability to deal with foreign powers on an equal basis. The bitterness exploded in revolution in 1911, and the Manchu dynasty, which had ruled in China since the seventeenth century, was overthrown.

☆ 5 ☆

No strong central government emerged to take its place. Local leaders, called "warlords," ruled areas of the country with private armies and resisted attempts to unify it. Decades of internal strife, revolution, and civil war would ensue, further weakening China.

Japan took advantage of the internal chaos in China. With the outbreak of World War I in 1914, the Western powers became preoccupied with events in Europe. Entering the war on the Allied side, Japan seized the German sphere of influence in the Shantung Peninsula. In 1915, the Japanese presented China with the Twenty-one Demands, which if accepted in full would have made China a Japanese protectorate.

The United States protested the Japanese demands. Diplomatic negotiations produced an American-Japanese agreement in November 1917. The United States recognized Japan's "special interests" in China, while Japan agreed to recognize the territorial sovereignty of China and "adhere to the principle of the so-called 'Open Door.' "

The American-Japanese agreement seemed contradictory to U.S. President Woodrow Wilson's espousal of the principle of self-determination. Wilson's Fourteen Points, outlined as a guide to an enduring peace, raised great hopes and expectations among the Chinese people. During the Versailles Peace Conference after World War I, however, Wilson was forced to compromise his principles to satisfy the other victorious nations, who demanded territorial rewards for their war efforts. The Chinese delegation at Versailles walked out in protest at the concessions granted, and refused to sign the treaty.

When the terms of the peace treaty were announced in 1919, the news that Japan had been given the German rights in the Shantung Peninsula produced outrage and a sense of betrayal in China. Young nationalistic students helped to organize demonstrations protesting the concessions. The May 4th Movement, which started in Peking, spread throughout the country. It helped produce a new leadership that would guide China's destiny for the next half century, and spurred Chinese determination to rid the country of foreign domination.

Throughout the 1920s, the United States continued its policy of the Open Door. In 1922, a conference of nations in Washington produced the Nine-Power Treaty, in which the signatories agreed to respect the sovereignty, independence, and territorial and administrative integrity of China; to provide the opportunity for China to develop and maintain an effective and stable government; to use their influence to establish and maintain the principle of equal opportunity for the commerce of all nations throughout the territory of China; and to refrain from taking advantage of conditions in China to seek special privileges and rights. Japan and the United States were among the signatories.

China accepted the Nine-Power Treaty but was disappointed in that it did not apply retroactively; China's request for revision of the "unequal treaties" was turned down. A future conference was to settle the issues of extraterritoriality and autonomy of the Chinese tariff, but no comprehensive action was taken. In addition, there was no machinery for implementation of the treaty, so that later, when Japan again encroached on China's territory, there was no means of stopping it.

THE CHINESE REPUBLIC

During the early 1920s, China's best-known leader was Sun Yat-sen. Sun had been one of the leaders of the Revolution of 1911 and was proclaimed first president of the Chinese Republic. He had been swept aside, but in the postwar period he renewed his efforts to unify China. After the war, Sun went to Canton, where he was one of the leaders governing the region. In 1921, a parliament elected him president of China. He tried to get support for his government from the Western powers, including the United States, but they continued to support a regime that was based in Peking.

Sun then turned to the Soviet Union. In 1923 Sun's government signed a treaty with the Soviets by which the Russians agreed to help organize Sun's governing party, the Kuomintang. There was also a fledgling Communist party in China; its members would be allowed into the Kuomintang while keeping their membership in the Communist party. The cooperation between the Kuomintang and the Communists was known as the United Front. The next year, the Soviet Union agreed to give up its special treaty rights in China, with the exception of railroad rights in Manchuria. The USSR was thus the first nation to do away with the "unequal treaty" rights that China resented. Soviet advisers soon came to China to organize the Kuomintang and help train the Chinese military forces.

After the death of Sun Yat-sen in 1925, leadership of the Kuomintang fell to his assistant, Chiang Kai-shek. In 1926, Chiang set out to unify the country through military force. Under his command, Kuomintang armies marched north to the Yangtze River. Warlord resistance collapsed and the cities of Nanchang and Wuhan were taken. In 1927, with military success within his grasp, Chiang turned against his Chinese Communist allies, destroying the United Front and wiping out the Communist party base in Shanghai.

Chiang continued his unification campaign, proclaiming the Republic of China with its capital at Nanking in 1928. His forces took Peking in 1929, and the United States recognized his government. But Chiang's control of China was never really complete. In many areas he ruled only with the cooperation of local warlords.

The Communists, after their defeat at Shanghai, held little enclaves within the country, most importantly in the Kiangsi and Hunan regions. Areas of Communist control were consolidated into the Chinese Soviet Republic in 1931, with Mao Tse-tung as chairman in the capital of Juichin.

**Sun Yat-sen, the first president
of the Chinese Republic,
in a photograph taken in 1923.**

Here, in embryo, was the birth of the "two-China" problem, which was to cause agonizing national debate in the United States years later.

Chiang launched a series of five "extermination campaigns" against the Communists. In the last of these, in 1934, using German military advisers, Chiang bottled up the Communist army around Kiangsi. The Communists broke out of the net and began a prolonged retreat known as the Long March.

Starting with 100,000 people, the Communists marched in the years 1934–35 some 6000 miles to a secure base in Shensi Province in the northwest of China, completing the march with a force of 30,000. Along the way, Mao consolidated his hold on the Communist forces in China. After establishing a capital at Yenan he continued to attract Communist followers from all over China.

JAPANESE AGGRESSION

In 1931, Japan used a trumped-up incident to invade Manchuria, setting up a protectorate known as Manchukuo in 1932. The United States' response to the new Japanese land grab in China was the strongest of any great power's; Secretary of State Henry L. Stimson declared that his government would not recognize territorial gains taken by force. But Stimson's protest carried no effective sanctions against the Japanese. The economic Depression had weakened the United States' willingness to intercede in faraway places.

The Japanese were not deterred from attacking the Jehol Province of China in 1933. Though the Chinese Communists had declared war on Japan the preceding year, Chiang effectively ceded the occupied areas to Japan by the Tangku Truce in May 1933.

Chiang was partly motivated by his continuing desire to stamp out the Communists, but his policies fanned discontent among his supporters. In December 1936, Chiang was kidnapped and held until he agreed to a second United Front with the Communists to fight the Japanese. The Communists promised to abandon the effort to overthrow the

Kuomintang government and agreed to stop confiscation of land in the zone it controlled. Mao adopted a policy of reducing rents to peasants for use of the land and also agreed to bring his army under the control of Chiang's government. In return, the Nanking regime was to undertake serious opposition to the Japanese, and introduce constitutional, social, and economic reforms.

The United Front was established none too soon. In July 1937, Japanese troops near the Marco Polo Bridge outside Peking provoked an incident with Chinese soldiers that led to all-out war between the two countries. This incident began the Asian phase of World War II.

Japanese forces quickly took Peking and Tientsin and then turned south toward Shanghai. In December they captured Chiang's capital at Nanking, in a campaign notable for the brutality of Japanese troops toward Chinese civilians. The "rape of Nanking" shocked the world.

In the fall of 1937, the Communist forces, starting from their base in Shensi Province, moved across the country to the sea in a four-month struggle. This action began the Communist guerrilla warfare behind Japanese lines and the establishment of Communist political bases in the north of China. From the countryside, Communist forces would continue to harass the Japanese throughout the war.

Chiang moved his capital to Hankow, but in April 1938, the Japanese moved against that as well. After the fall of Hankow, the Chinese government moved to Chungking, where it remained until the war's end.

By 1939 the Japanese army controlled all of the coast of China and much of the inland plains. In 1940 the Japanese established a puppet government at Nanking. As the lines stabilized and fighting ebbed in 1939, the United Front started to fade. Chiang was still suspicious of the objectives of the Communists, and as the threat of new Japanese offensives waned, he again attacked his Communist allies, in January 1941.

American reaction to the Japanese aggression in China was stated by President Franklin D. Roosevelt in a 1937 speech, in which he called for a "quarantine against aggression." Roosevelt's warning met a negative response from Americans. Isolationist feeling was strong and Americans feared being involved in another war. In December 1937, Japanese planes sank an American gunboat in the Yangtze River, but Roosevelt accepted a note of apology.

But the United States acted in other ways to oppose Japanese aggression. The government placed an embargo on the shipment of strategic materials to Japan, and in December 1938, the United States extended credit worth $25 million to China. The United States refused to recognize the Japanese puppet regime at Nanking.

Although Americans were reluctant to send military aid, they favored the Chinese cause. Chiang's brother-in-law, T. V. Soong, lobbied successfully in Washington for American aid. American lend-lease aid was extended to China in August 1941, and shortly afterward U.S. planes and volunteer airmen known as the "Flying Tigers" went to China to help protect the Burma Road, the chief supply route to Chiang's government.

U.S. ROLE IN CHINA
DURING WW II

On December 7, 1941, the Japanese attacked the American fleet at Pearl Harbor, Hawaii, and the United States declared war on Japan. Japan's European allies, Germany and Italy, then declared war on the United States, and the war in Europe and the war in Asia became one global war, in which priorities for allocation of war matériel, men, and weapons would have to be set. The military strategy of the war was decided almost immediately after Pearl Harbor at a joint U.S.–British chief of staff conference. Victory in Europe was to be the first priority. This decision meant that there would be very limited supplies for the China theater in the war.

Roosevelt had a romantic view of China, rooted in the tales his grandfather, a merchant in the China trade, had told him as a boy.

Roosevelt believed that in the postwar world, China would

play a vital role in the security of the Far East. He foresaw that after the defeat of Japan, China would be the major power in Asia. He hoped to build up Chinese military force both to help in the defeat of Japan and to enable Chiang to play a strong role in the postwar world.

Roosevelt was unaware of the real military situation within China. It had already weakened itself in four years of fighting with the Japanese. Chiang hoped that the United States would defeat Japan for him, allowing him to use his newly strengthened army for a future showdown with the Communists.

By the time the United States entered the war, it was the only power capable of giving military assistance to China. The Russians, who had been Chiang's major source of supplies, had to devote their energies to repulsing Hitler's attacks that began in 1941. In addition, the fall of Rangoon and the Burma Road to the Japanese had isolated China from the rest of the world.

Roosevelt sent General Joseph Stilwell to serve as chief of staff for Chiang in February 1942. Stilwell was assigned to coordinate efforts of Chinese, American, and British troops to reopen the Burma Road.

Chiang saw Stilwell as a threat to his own command. Stilwell was irked that Chiang seemed more concerned with the Communists than with the Japanese. Chiang kept his best forces to guard the area in the northwest where the Communists were strongest. Furthermore, the troops Chiang had on paper were often under the control of warlords with whom he had only a loose alliance. Chiang did not want to expose his weak position of leadership to Stilwell, and the two men developed a personal dislike.

Claire Chennault, who had been the adviser for Chiang's air force and was now commanding the U.S. air forces in China, suggested an alternative plan. He felt that massive bombing by U.S. planes could drive the Japanese from their positions in Burma. Chiang endorsed the plan, since it did not call for the use of Chinese troops, and Roosevelt began to build up American air power in China. But

☆ **13** ☆

Stilwell protested that air attacks would result in Japanese attempts to knock out the air bases in China.

The American public was not aware of the difficulties within China. American propaganda exaggerated the effect of its Chinese ally in the war effort. Chiang was portrayed as a popular democratic leader. The split of Chinese popular support between Chiang and the Communist forces was not publicized.

The year 1943 marked the high point of American support of Chiang. Roosevelt believed that the final assault on the Japanese home islands would have to come from Chinese bases. In January, FDR approved the U.S.–China Treaty which relinquished American claims to extraterritorial rights. At the end of the year, he signed a bill repealing the discriminatory legislation on immigration which had been in effect since the nineteenth century.

China's prestige was further enhanced when it was included in the Four-Power Declaration at Moscow in October, a joint agreement on the conduct of the war and the postwar settlement.

The most important recognition of Chiang's status was his inclusion with Roosevelt and British Prime Minister Winston Churchill at their meeting at Cairo. The resulting Cairo Declaration of December 1 called for the postwar return to China of all lands lost to Japan, including Manchuria and the offshore islands of Formosa and the Pescadores.

At the time of the Cairo Conference, Chinese support for the defeat of Japan was still regarded as being very important. At least twenty-three Japanese divisions were tied down in China, and there was a fear that if Chiang left the war, some of these Japanese forces would be freed for the island fighting in the Pacific.

**General and Mme. Chiang Kai-shek
posed with General Joseph Stilwell
in April 1942.**

☆ **15** ☆

Soon after, however, American successes in the Pacific brought American air bases close enough to begin the bombing of Japan. Thus, the importance of China as a strategic base faded, but Chiang's importance as an ally had played such an important role in Allied propaganda that the war in China required continued support.

Unfortunately, the air attacks on Japanese positions in China brought forth the response Stilwell had predicted. In February 1944, the Japanese launched another major assault within China. There was little effective resistance and the air bases on the mainland were soon overrun. Japanese forces threatened to take Chungking itself.

For a time Roosevelt backed Stilwell in his demands that Chiang be pressured to commit his troops strongly against the Japanese. In July 1944, Roosevelt sent Chiang a blunt note, asking that Stilwell be put in command of all Chinese troops and threatening to withhold further U.S. aid if Chiang refused.

Chiang was pushed against the wall. He saw the note as an attempt to violate his sovereignty, and he adopted his old policy of agreeing, but stalling the enforcement of the order. Chiang had let it be known that the real problem in the command of the China theater was Stilwell's abrasive personality.

For some time, reports from Stilwell and other Americans in China had informed Washington that the Communist Chinese were more effective at fighting the Japanese than were Chiang's disorganized and badly led forces. Stilwell was upset that much of the aid to Chiang that was intended for use against the Japanese was instead used to supply troops that opposed the Communists in the North.

U.S. MEDIATION EFFORTS

By 1944, reports of the strength of the Communists were causing concern in Washington. In June 1944, FDR had sent Vice-President Henry Wallace on a fact-finding mission to China. Wallace urged Chiang to coordinate his efforts with the Communists, a proposal that Chiang temporarily agreed to, while warning that the Communists should not be regarded as mere "agrarian reformers."

In July 1944, an American observer team went to the Communist headquarters at Yenan. Calling themselves the "Dixie Mission" because they were in "rebel" territory, these Americans were favorably impressed with the fighting spirit of Mao's troops and the obvious popularity of his government. "We have come into a different country and are meeting a different people," reported Foreign Service officer John S. Service.

Service had an eight-hour talk with Mao, in which Mao stated his attitude toward the Soviet Union and the United States. The Communist chief said:

We Communists accepted Kuomintang terms in 1936–37 to form the United Front because the foreign menace of Japan threatened the country. We are, first of all, Chinese. . . .

Soviet participation . . . in China's post-war reconstruction depends entirely on the circumstances of the Soviet Union. The Russians have suffered greatly in the war and will have their hands full with their own job of rebuilding. We do not expect Russian help. . . .

But Russia will not oppose American interests in China if they are constructive and democratic. There will be no possible point of conflict. Russia only wants a friendly and democratic China. Cooperation between America and the Chinese Communist Party will be beneficial and satisfactory to all concerned. . . .

China must industrialize. This can be done—in China —only by free enterprise and with the aid of foreign capital. Chinese and American interests are correlated and similar. They fit together, economically and politically. We can and must work together. . . .

We will not be afraid of democratic American influence—we will welcome it . . .

America does not need to fear that we will not be

cooperative. We must cooperate and we must have American help. This is why it is so important to us Communists to know what you Americans are thinking and planning. We cannot risk crossing you—cannot risk any conflict with you.

Soon after the Wallace trip, Roosevelt sent Major General Patrick J. Hurley to China to investigate the disagreement between Chiang and General Stilwell. On the way, Hurley stopped in Moscow to confer with Soviet Foreign Minister Vyacheslav Molotov. Molotov assured Hurley that the Russians had no interest in a Communist take-over of China.

Hurley was the answer to Chiang's hopes. The quick-tempered Hurley had no previous experience in China, and believed Chiang's argument that Stilwell was a major obstacle to the Chinese war effort. Stilwell's warnings were now taken less seriously, for the Japanese offensive had petered out. Hurley's reports swayed Roosevelt, and in October 1944, Stilwell was replaced by General Albert C. Wedemeyer.

Though China was by now less important militarily because it was no longer needed as a base from which to launch attacks on Japan, the question of postwar China still loomed. Some Foreign Service officials such as John Paton Davies accepted the reality that the Communists were firmly entrenched in the north and that it was in the American interest to come to some accommodation with Mao along with Chiang.

For the present, the United States sought to reconcile the two opposing sides in China. Roosevelt sent Hurley to Yenan to try to arrange an effective alliance between Mao and Chiang. The proposals arising from Hurley's meeting with Mao included reorganization of Chiang's national government into a coalition government, and a national military council under a united command in which the Communists would be represented. The Communists were to share in foreign aid.

Hurley endorsed these proposals, and flew back to Chung-king with Mao's aide, Chou En-lai, to present them to Chiang. Chiang turned them down, insisting that the Communists surrender their armies to his control and accept posts in his government. Chou, remembering Chiang's previous attacks on the Communists, could not accept this. Efforts to reach a compromise continued.

In February 1945, Roosevelt went to Yalta to meet with Stalin and Churchill. Roosevelt wanted Stalin's commitment to enter the war against the Japanese. Though secret work on the U.S. atomic bomb was proceeding, there was no guarantee it would be completed in time to defeat Japan. Russia was granted special postwar economic concessions in Manchuria, such as railway and port rights. Stalin, in turn, agreed to recognize Chiang's regime as the sole government of China. Chiang was told of the Yalta agreements in June by Hurley.

On August 6, 1945, the United States dropped an atomic bomb on Japan. Three days later, the Soviet Union entered the war against Japan, invading Manchuria on the same day. On the fourteenth, the Soviets signed a treaty with Chiang's government ratifying the Russian concessions in Manchuria that had been given at Yalta. The Japanese surrendered the same day, but in China, fighting continued —the final struggle between Chiang and Mao for control of China.

CIVIL WAR

The defeat of Japan did not settle the question of who was to rule China. Under Chiang the Nationalists' military position was now more vulnerable than in 1937. While the Communist Chinese forces were spread out over a large area from Shensi Province to Shantung, the Nationalists were confined to western China. From 1937 to 1945, the Communists increased their military forces from 85,000 to about 1 million. In 1937 they controlled areas with a total population of only 1.5 million; by 1945 they occupied areas with a total of about 90 million population. The Communists had a strong grass-roots organization, a secure base, and battle-hardened forces with years of experience fighting a guerrilla war against the Japanese.

On the other hand, the Nationalist regime was recognized as the sole national government of China by both the United States and the Soviet Union. During the war, the Nationalists had received about $1.5 billion in U.S. aid, and more aid followed after the war's end. That aid had helped to build and equip an army of about 3 million men, some of whom had been American trained. Chiang hoped that when the Russians withdrew from Manchuria, they would turn over this key industrial area to him, as promised.

But the Nationalists faced many problems. Corruption within the Kuomintang had increased during the war. Horrendous wartime inflation had lessened the value of the government-issued currency. By September 1945, the volume of paper money had increased 465 times since July 1937. With the retaking of areas that had been under Japanese control, China's economy improved, but even worse inflation was to come.

To strengthen his position, Chiang insisted that all Japanese forces surrender to his troops alone. The Chinese Communists argued that those Chinese troops nearest Japanese positions should take the surrender. Given the Communists' strategic location, this would have been tantamount to giving control of north China to Mao's forces.

THE U.S. FAVORS
THE NATIONALISTS

The new American president, Harry Truman, decided the issue in favor of the wartime ally. He ordered the Japanese troops to surrender only to the Nationalists. Mao charged American interference in the Chinese internal struggle.

American soldiers, airmen, technicians, administrators, and other civilian advisers in China helped enforce the Japanese surrender to the Nationalists. American planes and ships transported Nationalist troops to the Yangtze coastal cities, and north to the main urban areas of Peking and Tientsin. Some 60,000 American marines were brought from the Pacific to secure vital railroad lines and airfields in north China. American marines took over the city of Tientsin until Nationalist forces could arrive.

In some areas, Japanese troops were ordered to fight off the Communist forces in order to hold their positions for the Nationalists. To facilitate the surrender, Japanese troops withdrew into cities, leaving the countryside unoccupied. Communist troops moved into the areas the Japanese had left, and fighting between Communists and Nationalists ensued.

The United States was aware of the difficulties that the two struggling groups posed for its postwar foreign policy. Wedemeyer warned that the Nationalists could win control of a united China only with the aid of American troops—something a war-weary nation would not support. Yet the other alternative, as Wedemeyer saw it, was U.S. disengagement from China—in effect allowing the civil war to run its course, while continuing to send supplies to Chiang. Under this option, Wedemeyer thought Chiang would be able to stabilize south China; the Communists would hold north China and Manchuria.

Truman wanted China united, as a strong obstacle not only to Japan but to Soviet expansionism in Asia. He continued to press for a negotiated settlement between Mao and Chiang. The talks between the two sides, mediated by Hurley, continued intermittently but without success.

In November, Ambassador Hurley returned to the United States and offered his resignation. At a press conference, Hurley blamed Foreign Service officials for the failure of his mission. He charged: "The professional Foreign Service men sided with the Chinese Communist armed party and the imperialist bloc of nations whose policy it was to keep China divided against herself."

THE MARSHALL MEDIATION EFFORT

Truman was angered by Hurley's charges of disloyalty in the State Department, and accepted his resignation. He then asked General George C. Marshall, who had been chief of staff of the U.S. Army during the war, to go to China to negotiate a cease-fire between the two sides and act as mediator for negotiations toward a united and democratic China.

Marshall commanded enormous respect, and his presence in China soon brought results. A conference with both Nationalist and Communist leaders in Chungking in January

1946 resulted in three major agreements announced by the end of February. The first established a military truce, with both sides remaining in their present areas of control. Three-member truce teams, including American, Nationalist, and Communist representatives, would enforce the truce. A second agreement set up a policymaking State Council, in which the Kuomintang, the Communists, and other parties would share power. This council would provide for the establishment of a national legislature. Finally, a military reorganization would eventually incorporate the Communist armies into a national army. American military missions were sent to both Nationalist and Communist forces to help supervise the transition.

Events in Manchuria soon threatened these agreements, however. The Soviets surrendered the major cities and railroad lines to the Nationalists as promised. But the departing Russian troops permitted Mao's forces to obtain some arms and equipment left by the Japanese. Fighting broke out between the two sides when the Communists moved in more troops than the agreement allowed and the Nationalists refused to allow the truce teams to operate.

In July the Nationalists violated the truce and waged an all-out offensive in Manchuria. In October, Nationalist troops captured Kalgan, northwest of Peking.

Marshall continued to try and mediate a settlement, but was unable to get either side to make concessions. Truman warned Chiang that unless the Nationalists followed a policy of reform, the United States would reconsider its support for him. Chiang regarded this as an empty threat. His brother-in-law, T. V. Soong, informed him that public support in the United States was behind the Nationalist government and Truman had no choice but to continue American aid.

In a December meeting with Chiang, Marshall warned him that the Chinese Communist forces were too strong to be defeated militarily, and that Chiang must seek a political solution to the dispute. Chiang's noncommittal response convinced Marshall there was nothing more he could do in China, and he requested his recall on December 28. On his return in January, he blamed the failure of his mission on both contending sides in China.

Marshall was named secretary of state, and his appointment received not one dissenting vote in the Senate confirmation. Most Americans thought his China task had been an impossible one, and that he should not be blamed for the failure.

THE NATIONALIST PUSH
FOR VICTORY

At the beginning of 1947, a Nationalist victory seemed possible. In February, Chiang publicly blamed the United States for prolonging the fighting by holding up credit and arms during Marshall's mediation efforts. He began a new offensive in the Shantung Peninsula. In March, Nationalist troops took Yenan, and Chiang told the American ambassador, John Leighton Stuart, that the Communists would be defeated by the autumn. In May, Truman resumed U.S. military aid to the Nationalist regime.

Chiang had many supporters in the United States, known as the "China Lobby," who put pressure on the administration to step up its aid to the Nationalists. One of the most influential Nationalist sympathizers was the magazine publisher Henry R. Luce, himself the son of American missionaries in China, and a close friend of Chiang. In Luce's magazine *Life* in October 1947, American diplomat William C. Bullitt charged that the administration was not doing enough to keep China out of the hands of Stalin.

Bullitt charged that Roosevelt had betrayed China at Yalta and proposed that the United States make amends by investing more than $1 billion over the next three years in China and sending advisers to supervise reform. Bullitt further wrote: ". . . one of the first acts of Congress when it reconvenes should be an investigation of our policies with regard to China. Such an investigation might at least fix responsibilities and reveal the names of the men in our government and Foreign Service who are incompetent to preserve the vital interests of the people of the U.S."

In conclusion Bullitt predicted: "The cause is a common cause. If China falls into the hands of Stalin, all Asia, including Japan, sooner or later will fall into his hands. The manpower and resources of Asia will be mobilized against us. The independence of the U.S. will not live a generation longer than the independence of China." Like many Americans, Bullitt assumed that Mao would be merely a puppet ruler of the Soviet regime.

In July, the U.S. government sent General Wedemeyer back to China to report on the military situation. He recognized that the Communist program of land and social reform brought widespread popular support for the Communist cause. Wedemeyer made a secret report to Truman in which he advised large-scale "moral, advisory, and material support" for the Nationalists, provided that Chiang instituted economic and political reforms. He advised that Manchuria be put under a five-year guardianship of the United Nations.

Truman continued to send aid to China, totaling more than $2 billion between 1945 and 1949, but he was reluctant to provide troops to support the Nationalist struggle. There were several reasons for his reluctance. All competent military advice warned against the United States becoming involved in a land war in Asia. There was also the possibility that the use of American troops would bring a Soviet military response.

The crucial factor was that Truman's foreign policy was chiefly concerned with containing Soviet aggression in Europe. The Truman Doctrine and the Marshall Plan gave military and economic aid to prevent the spread of Communism. In the State Department, George Kennan, one of the authors of the containment policy, argued successfully that the center of the Cold War lay in Europe. Since resources were limited and American strategic thinking placed the Far East low in priority, the bulk of American aid went to Europe.

THE TIDE TURNS

The military situation in China was more dangerous than it appeared to Chiang. Mao's policy was to avoid a major battle unless he was certain of victory. Despite Chiang's early successes, the Communists were building toward a victory that, when it came, would be shockingly swift.

In the countryside, Mao's People's Liberation Army was consolidating its support among the peasants. Gradually, Mao isolated the city strongholds. In December 1947, Mao announced that the "turning point has been reached."

Communist offensives early in 1948 retook Yenan and the city of Kaifeng, midway between Peking and Chungking. By November the Communists controlled all of Manchuria. The American embassy at Nanking reported that in four major battles the Nationalists had lost 33 divisions and 33,000 men, most of whom had been equipped with American arms.

In November 1948, General David Barr of the American Military Advisory Group in China reported to the Department of the Army, "I am convinced that the military situation has deteriorated to the point where only active participation of U.S. troops could effect a remedy. . . . [The Nationalists'] debacles in my opinion can all be attributed to the world's worst leadership and many other morale-destroying factors that can lead to a complete loss of will to fight. The complete ineptness of high military leaders and the widespread corruption and dishonesty throughout the armed forces, could, in some measure, have been controlled and directed had the . . . authority and facilities been available. Chinese leaders lack the moral courage to issue and enforce an unpopular decision." Barr recommended the removal of the U.S. Military Advisory Group from China.

Pessimistic appraisals such as Wedemeyer's and Barr's were not released to the American public. Secretary of State Marshall was afraid that revealing the real situation would constitute "a knock-out blow to the Nationalist government." But concealing the true situation, combined with the arguments of the China Lobby, made Chiang's ultimate fall more shocking than it should have been.

China was an issue in the American elections of 1948. The China Lobby found support among business-minded conservatives, who were encouraged by Soong's promises of favorable market concessions in a "free China." Chiang expected that a Republican victory would result in greater aid for his government. But Truman's surprise victory guaranteed there would be no increased American involvement.

By the end of 1948, the Chinese economy was in a state of collapse. Nationalist troops were defecting en masse. The United States advised its citizens in Nanking to leave. Major Nationalist defeats in November and December made the outcome of the war a foregone conclusion.

Desperate, Chiang sent his wife to Washington to appeal for more aid. In March 1949, fifty senators asked the president to approve a $1.5 billion loan to the Nationalists. When the administration replied that American weapons were being captured by the Communists almost as soon as they reached China, the request was pared down to $75 million. This aid was eventually sent to prevent starvation on Formosa after Chiang had withdrawn there.

The Communist advance was inexorable. In January 1949, Peking and Tientsin fell to the People's Liberation Army. Chiang shifted his government to Canton before Nanking fell in April. When the Communists captured Shanghai in May, the Nationalists ordered its port closed to shipping. American ships helped enforce the blockade, and even stood by as American merchant ships were shelled by the Nationalists. The blockade held until Soviet fighter planes appeared in February 1950 to protect the city from Nationalist bombers, based by that time on Formosa.

On October 1, 1949, Mao declared the establishment of the People's Republic of China. On the fifteenth, Canton fell and the Nationalist capital shifted to Chungking and then to Chengtu. Finally, in December, the Nationalists fled to the offshore island of Formosa. (Formosa, as the island was called in the 1950's, was a Portuguese name; later the island was commonly known by its Chinese name, Taiwan.) The Communists now controlled mainland China.

Secretary of State Dean Acheson took on the task of explaining Chiang's defeat to the American people. The State Department issued a "White Paper" in August 1949, tracing Chinese-American relations. It charged that Chiang's government had been unable to govern effectively and that Chiang's mistakes, not lack of American aid, had brought on his defeat.

But 1949 was a watershed year. The year before, Communist aggression in Europe had taken a more active form with the Berlin blockade and the take-over of Czechoslovakia. American newspapers in 1949 were filled with accusations that a high State Department officer, Alger Hiss, was a Communist agent. The explosion of an atomic bomb by the Russians in September 1949, breaking the U.S. nuclear monopoly, raised new fears. Mao's victory, which Americans had not expected, caused bitterness and shock and led to charges that the administration had not only been wrong, but harbored traitors. The question "Who lost China?" became part of a national debate that poisoned American politics for years.

That China was not America's to lose occurred to few. Most Americans saw a vast, monolithic Communist coalition stretching from Berlin to Pyongyang (in North Korea). Mao further confirmed American fears in July, 1949 with his statement that his government would "lean to one side" to support the forces of socialism against those of imperialism. In December, Mao went to Moscow and in February 1950, a Sino-Soviet alliance was announced.

Despite domestic criticism, Truman's administration seemed to be making attempts to recognize the reality of a Chinese Communist government. In a covering letter to the White Paper, Acheson offered the People's Republic of China the "traditional support for the Open Door," a proposal that Mao scorned.

Nonetheless, the United States remained unwilling to send troops to defend the remnants of Chiang's forces on Formosa. On January 3, 1950, the State Department notified its embassies that the fall of Formosa was to be expected.

In a speech on January 5, Truman said that Formosa was part of China and that no military aid or advisers would go to it. In another speech, Acheson excluded both Formosa and Korea from the essential defense perimeter of the United States.

But a frightening new development united Americans into a rigid China policy. In June 1950, North Korean troops crossed the 38th parallel that divided Korea into north and south, and swept down the Korean Peninsula. The Korean War began, with enduring results for China and the United States.

ISOLATION
AND
CONTAINMENT

The American policy of noninvolvement in the Chinese civil war came to an end with the Korean invasion. President Truman immediately made the decision to resist Communist aggression with force. Two days after the initial attack, he ordered the U.S. Seventh Fleet into the Formosa Strait, and declared that "the occupation of Formosa by Communist forces would be a direct threat to the security of the Pacific area. . . ."

The following day, Chou En-lai declared that the American actions were "aggression against the territory of China. . . . It is precisely a further act of intervention by American imperialism in the affairs of Asia."

UNITED NATIONS INVOLVEMENT

On June 27, with the Soviet Union's delegate boycotting the UN Security Council over the issue of recognition of mainland China, the United Nations passed a resolution calling for military assistance to protect South Korea's independence. Though most of the troops and commanders of the

UN force were American, they would fight under a United Nations flag.

General Douglas MacArthur was picked to head the UN force. MacArthur's public statements about the conduct of the war often went further than Truman wanted, and at times he seemed to be trying to make American foreign policy. MacArthur conferred with Chiang on Taiwan in August 1950 and called for Taiwan's being turned into a U.S. defensive stronghold. Truman asked that the statement be withdrawn. It was, but it added to the fears of the People's Republic of China that American intentions were not only to defend Korea, but to retake China.

On September 15, MacArthur led the UN troops in a brilliant amphibious landing at the port of Inchon. The North Korean forces were pushed back to the 38th parallel. MacArthur asked for and received permission to cross the line and destroy the North Korean forces.

Truman could hardly refuse the demands of the hero who was "rolling back the iron curtain," but as MacArthur's forces neared the Yalu River border between China and Korea, the Chinese Communists became alarmed. Chou sent warnings that the Chinese would not "stand idly by" if the United States tried to destroy North Korea. Truman and MacArthur met in October at Wake Island in mid-Pacific, and MacArthur assured the president that the military situation was well in hand. Even at this time, however, Chinese "volunteers" had made probes south of the Yalu River.

In November, Chinese Communist troops swept across the border with numbers and strength for which MacArthur was unprepared. Bitter, bloody fighting failed to stem the tide as MacArthur's forces were pushed back in the longest retreat in American military history. By December 15 the line of battle was again south of the 38th parallel.

After the strength of the Chinese onslaught became clear, MacArthur asked for bombers to attack the Chinese bases north of the Yalu, in Manchuria. Truman refused, fearing to widen the war with an action that might require greater numbers of American troops. The U.S.'s European allies

**General Douglas MacArthur and President Harry Truman
met on Wake Island in October 1950,
to discuss America's policy in the Far East.**

feared that a wider war in Asia would draw American commitments away from Europe and leave the way open for Stalin's forces to advance there.

In December an American magazine published MacArthur's opinion that Truman's orders not to attack Manchuria were "an enormous handicap." MacArthur warned that American forces were in danger of complete defeat. A Chinese-Soviet alliance, he said, could demand that the United States abandon Formosa and allow Communist Chinese involvement in the Japanese peace treaty, still unsigned. That could keep the United States from establishing bases in Japan and open the way to Communist takeover of the Far East.

Through speeches and leaks of important information to antiadministration Republicans in Congress, MacArthur continued to attack Truman. MacArthur told House Republican leader Joseph W. Martin, Jr., "If we lose the war to Communism in Asia, the fall of Europe is inevitable; win it and Europe most probably would avoid war and yet preserve freedom." MacArthur felt that the Chinese Communists were already extended to the limits of their capability. He discounted the argument that an attack on China would bring the Soviet Union into the war.

Truman disagreed, feeling that the United States could not afford to get bogged down in a land war against the Chinese. Furthermore, he felt that MacArthur's statements were undermining his prerogative as president to set U.S. foreign policy. On April 11, 1951, Truman relieved MacArthur from command.

The dismissal caused a furor. MacArthur returned home to public acclaim, a ticker tape parade in New York City, and an invitation to address a joint session of Congress. To many Americans, Truman's actions confirmed the Republican charges that the Democrats were protecting traitors in the government.

U.S. SEARCH FOR SCAPEGOATS

Within the administration, the attitude toward China hardened. Military aid to the Nationalists resumed. Truman's quick response in June 1950 was prompted by the policy of containment and the fear that a Communist success would encourage further Communist aggression in Europe. As the war in Korea went on, American strategic thinking changed so that by the middle of 1951, the National Security Council decided that the "most immediate threats to U.S. security" were in Asia, not Europe.

The Communist Chinese were regarded as merely Russian tools. Dean Rusk, then an assistant secretary of state, wrote: "The peace and security of China are being sacrificed to the ambitions of a Communist conspiracy. China has been driven by foreign masters into an adventure of foreign aggression. . . . The Peiping regime may be a colonial, Russian government. . . . It is not the government of China. . . . It is not Chinese." (Rusk's use of the term "Peiping" for the Chinese capital became standard usage during the fifties and sixties. "Peking" means "northern capital," and the U.S. use of "Peiping," or "northern peace," reflected the view that the legitimate capital was still Chiang's old capital at Nanking.)

The Chinese defeat of American troops in battle caused consternation. In the search for an explanation, it was easier to believe that MacArthur had his hands tied by traitors in the State Department than that an invasion of China would have been dangerous. General Omar Bradley of the Joint Chiefs of Staff testified that a full-scale war with China would be "the wrong war, at the wrong place, at the wrong time, and with the wrong enemy," but the hunt for "traitors" went on.

Chief among those who raised the cry, "Who lost China?" and answered "Traitors!" was Senator Joseph R. McCarthy of Wisconsin. In February 1950, McCarthy gave his famous speech in Wheeling, West Virginia, in which he claimed to have a list of "card-carrying Communists" within the State Department. He followed this speech with others, charging initially that John S. Service, the man who had praised the Communist Chinese in his role as observer with the Dixie Mission, was one of the men responsible for the U.S.'s losing China.

McCarthy and his allies went on to attack most of the Foreign Service officers who had seen early on—too early—that Mao was stronger and Chiang weaker than Americans had been led to believe. Their warnings of a possible Nationalist defeat were interpreted as being the cause of Chiang's defeat and the Communist victory. The members of the Dixie Mission, who had been sent to meet with Mao at Yenan, were accused of consorting with known Communists.

The McCarthyites led a search for anyone in the government or out who might at any time have been a Communist or have been associated with Communist "fronts"—groups that were not openly Communist but were suspected of having Communist backing or large numbers of Communist members. Lists of suspected "fronts" and their memberships were drawn up. In the political climate of the fifties, any accusation of Communist membership or "leanings" was tantamount to a conviction of treason, and many patriotic Americans lost their jobs and reputations because of unfounded charges. McCarthy even attacked General Marshall.

Dwight Eisenhower's landslide victory in the 1952 presidential campaign was cemented by his promise to go to Korea. Truce talks had been carried on intermittently since mid-1951, and the country was tired of the war, which eventually cost 150,000 American casualties. On July 27, 1953, an armistice was signed, with a boundary between North and South Korea at virtually the same place as before the war.

POST-KOREAN U.S. POLICY

Though the Korean conflict was over, its effects on American policy toward China would endure for another twenty years. Eisenhower's new secretary of state, John Foster Dulles, expanded the containment policy to the point of declaring that Chiang's government was still the sole government of China. On Formosa, this fiction was carried out with a legislature including representatives from each of the mainland provinces, despite the fact that they were all under the control of the People's Republic.

☆ **35** ☆

In the "witch-hunts" for Communist sympathizers, neither Truman nor his successor defended those in the State Department's Far Eastern Division who had recommended an American accommodation with Mao. Though their advice had clearly not been followed, these men were hounded out of government and sometimes out of the country, though none were ever convicted of crimes. By the mid-fifties there were few people remaining in the State Department with long experience in China, and those who remained learned to follow the "hard line" against the People's Republic. The most promising and talented career officers in the Foreign Service field avoided specializing in China affairs.

Containment of the Chinese Communist regime was one of the aims of the U.S.–Japanese Peace Treaty of 1951, which Dulles had helped negotiate. By the terms of the treaty, Japan recognized the Nationalists as the representative of China, and agreed to the establishment of American bases on Japanese territory.

Further containment moves included a mutual defense treaty between the United States and South Korea in 1953 that allowed more American bases in Korea. In September 1954, Dulles organized the Southeast Asia Treaty Organization (SEATO), a bloc of non-Communist countries intended to serve as a regional defense alliance similar to the North Atlantic Treaty Organization (NATO) alliance between the United States and Western Europe.

In December 1954, though the Communists had held control of the mainland for five years, the United States tied itself to the proposition that the Nationalists were the sole legal government of China—a policy that would work against U.S. prestige in years to come. By signing a mutual defense treaty with the Nationalist regime, the United States committed itself to the defense of Formosa and the Pescadores if they were attacked.

In the treaty, ratified February 9, 1955, the United States also agreed to defend "such other territories as may be determined by mutual agreement"—a clause that would result in American debate over how far the United States was committed. Article 10 of the treaty said, "This treaty shall remain in force indefinitely. Either party may terminate it one year after notice has been given to the other party." Almost a quarter of a century would go by before this clause was invoked to allow the United States to normalize relations with Communist China.

Besides active containment, the U.S. policy of nonrecognition of the People's Republic included attempts to isolate the government of mainland China from participation in the world community. The primary means of isolation was refusing admission of the People's Republic into the United Nations, on the grounds that the world body had condemned it as an aggressor. A frequently heard slogan was, "Red China cannot shoot its way into the United Nations."

In addition, the United States enforced exclusion of the People's Republic from most international conferences and scientific, cultural, and educational meetings. "Red China" was excluded from the Olympics due to American influence with the International Olympic Committee. United States citizens were not allowed to travel to China for any purpose, even though their passports were good for travel to the Soviet Union—the supposed puppet master of China.

Most damaging of all the attempts to isolate China was the trade embargo enforced by the United States. Not only were American firms forbidden to send goods to the mainland, but no European or Japanese firm could do business in the United States if it traded in China.

In secret, the U.S. Central Intelligence Agency (CIA), headed by John Foster Dulles's brother Allen, carried out covert actions against the People's Republic. The agency cooperated with the Nationalists in raids and sabotage on the mainland. It even trained Tibetan guerrillas in Colorado for possible use in China. News stories about the CIA's provocative activities were denounced as Communist propaganda.

The American policy of containment and isolation led to a defensive and insular world view on the part of the Chinese. The People's Republic saw itself surrounded by enemies, including Formosa and Japan, that were supported with American aid and alliances. At the hands of the United States and its allies, China had suffered approximately one million casualties in the Korean War, including the death of Mao's son. The leaders of the mainland bombarded the Chinese people with propaganda portraying America as an aggressor, an imperialist, and the chief enemy of China. Mao expelled or imprisoned foreign missionaries. American prisoners captured during the Korean War were harshly treated and brainwashed, hardening American public opinion against the Communists.

For all the fear its rhetoric and actions caused, China was still an underdeveloped nation ravaged by Japanese occupation and civil war. The trade embargo cut it off from technology and manufactured goods that it needed to develop a strong economy. Trade with the Soviet Union was not a satisfactory substitute.

The China Lobby confidently predicted that the American policy of isolation would soon bring the Chinese Communists to their knees. In 1951, *Time* magazine reported, "Red China is in deep trouble. Early enthusiasm for the Red regime has turned to sullen resentment, distrust, and despair. . . . Mao is aging (59) and ailing (heart trouble), is obviously unable to wield as much personal power as he once had."

But Chiang's aggressive statements about reconquering the mainland often were an embarrassment to U.S. policymakers, who had to prop up his regime with aid just to enable him to keep Formosa. Chiang had actually been given free rein in 1953, only to be restricted again the following year when it became clear his proposed assault on the mainland would bring a Communist Chinese response that would require massive American aid and perhaps involve U.S. troops in the fighting.

FORMOSA STRAIT CRISES

In November 1954, the People's Republic announced that eleven captured U.S. Air Force pilots would be denied status as prisoners of war, but were to be jailed for war crimes. Against this background, Chiang and the People's Republic began shelling each other across the Formosa Strait.

Congress passed the Formosa Resolution of January 24, 1955, which gave the president authorization "to employ the armed forces of the United States as he deems necessary for the specific purpose of securing and protecting Formosa and the Pescadores against armed attack, this authority to include the securing and protection of such related positions and territories of that area now in friendly hands and the taking of such other measures as he judges to be required or appropriate in assuring the defense of Formosa and the Pescadores." Eisenhower, and his successors, were thus given a blank check to support any action they might want to take in the defense of Formosa.

In an attempt to calm tensions, the United Nations invited the Communist Chinese to send a delegation to discuss a cease-fire in the Formosa Strait. Mao refused, except on the condition that the Nationalists be "driven out of the Security Council." Chou accused the United States of "using war threats, brandishing atomic weapons to force the Chinese people into tolerating" the "occupation" of Taiwan.

The shelling in the Formosa Strait involved the islands of Quemoy and Matsu. The Pescadores are 90 miles (145 km) off the Chinese mainland, but tiny Quemoy (actually three islands) and Matsu were only 1 to 3 miles (1.6 to 4.8 km) from the mainland. They were held by Chiang, but were not specifically covered in the Mutual Defense Treaty.

Democratic Senator Estes Kefauver, in a speech on March 30, 1955, said that U.S. involvement in a war over "Matsu and Quemoy ought to be unthinkable." Senate Democratic Majority Leader Lyndon Johnson accused Republicans of "talking war."

But hard-liners in the United States insisted that the islands be defended as fiercely as Formosa itself. Republican Minority Leader William Knowland said that the Democrats wanted the United States to go "marching down the hill again in the face of Communist threats."

The actions taken by the United States kept the People's Republic from attempting to take the islands by force, and as the year 1955 went on, a de facto cease-fire lessened tensions in the Formosa Strait. The Communist Chinese did an abrupt about-face and offered to negotiate directly with the United States "to discuss the question of relaxing tension in the Far East and especially the question of relaxing tension in the Taiwan area."

The United States responded cautiously, saying it would always welcome sincere efforts to reach peace. Formal meetings with the Communist Chinese had to be treated gingerly, lest they be interpreted as de facto recognition of the People's Republic as the legitimate government of China. The United States asked that the People's Republic declare an immediate cease-fire and release the American airmen. A formal offer of talks would have to be conducted through a third party, and the Nationalists would have to be represented in any talks.

At the end of May, the People's Republic released four American airmen, and Chou repeated his offer to negotiate with the United States. Eleven other captured airmen were released on July 31. In a speech to the National People's Congress on July 30, Chou accused the United States of "interference with the liberation of China's coastal islands, and repeated the claim that the liberation of Formosa was "a matter of China's internal affairs." Yet he did promise the peaceful liberation of Formosa and offered to negotiate with Chiang's government—an offer which Chiang could never accept. (Ironically, when President Jimmy Carter eventually agreed on normalization terms twenty-four years later, he was not able to extract the same favorable concessions.)

Ambassadorial-level talks between the United States and the People's Republic began on August 1, 1955. Except for further agreements on the repatriation of American civilians held in China, the talks produced no gains.

The crisis, however, had been successfully defused without the loss of any Nationalist territory. Secretary of State Dulles claimed a victory for his policy of "brinkmanship," which he outlined in an article in Life in January 1956. Dulles revealed that Eisenhower had forced the Chinese Communists to come to the peace table over Korea by threatening to attack Chinese bases in Manchuria and employ tactical nuclear weapons. Similarly, the People's Republic had backed down over the Formosa Strait crisis because the United States had shown its willingness to go to war.

The danger in this policy was that the United States had to walk a tightrope carefully between its ally, Chiang, and the People's Republic. Chiang's warlike posture always carried the danger that he would embroil the United States in a war that would not be in the U.S.'s interests.

Another crisis over the Taiwan Strait arose in August 1958. Propaganda by both sides had hardened their positions, and on August 23, the Communists began artillery bombardment on the three islands grouped under the name Quemoy. Chiang had assembled some 90,000 troops, one third of his total forces, on these islands. The Nationalist troop buildup heightened Chinese Communist fears of an invasion, and served to increase the strategic importance of the islands.

Dulles again responded with clear threats of force. An amphibious force of 1600 marines was sent to the area. On the 27th, Eisenhower told a news conference that the offshore islands were more important to Formosa than they had been three years earlier, but declined to declare that the United States would defend them.

On the 29th, the mainland Chinese demanded the surrender of the Quemoys, declaring their intention to invade them. U.S. naval forces went to the area, escorting Nationalist supply ships, though keeping clear of the 3-mile (4.8 km) limit off the mainland. On September 5, the USSR said it would "aid Red China with all possible means at its disposal," just as if its own fate were being decided. Once again, the world seemed to be drawing closer to nuclear war on the issue of China.

A Gallup poll released September 26 showed that 91 percent of informed Americans preferred turning the Quemoy-Matsu issue over to the UN rather than committing American forces to Chiang's defense.

**A Nationalist Chinese Army soldier is able to get
a clear view of mainland China from Quemoy Island.**

The United States and the People's Republic resumed ambassadorial talks in Warsaw on September 15. The Communists agreed to a partial halt in the bombardment; in return the United States agreed to halt the naval escorts of supply ships. In October, Dulles flew to Formosa for talks with Chiang. On October 23, they issued a joint announcement stating that the Nationalists had renounced force as a means of regaining the mainland. Though this policy had been secretly agreed on since 1954, and Dulles had reported it in secret to a Senate committee in 1955, it had never been publicly announced. The People's Republic attacks tapered off. Quemoy and Matsu remained in the hands of the Nationalists.

Dulles claimed another victory for brinkmanship. Critics charged that Quemoy and Matsu had not been worth the risk of nuclear war.

In the presidential elections of 1960, Eisenhower's vice-president, Richard M. Nixon, who was the Republican nominee, met the Democratic candidate, Senator John F. Kennedy, in a series of televised debates. One of the issues raised was the defense of Quemoy and Matsu. Kennedy indicated he would yield them to concentrate on the defense of Formosa. Nixon declared that no area of freedom should be relinquished to the Communists. Kennedy softened his stand, but neither man seriously questioned the main thrust of U.S. policy toward China.

Indeed, the victorious Kennedy's choice of the fervently anti-Communist Dean Rusk for his secretary of state indicated a continuance of the Eisenhower-Dulles China policy. Kennedy would continue nonrecognition of the People's Republic of China, opposition to its entry into the United Nations, military and economic support for Formosa, and readiness to come to the aid of any country that seemed threatened by Communist take-over. This last policy would lead to American involvement in Vietnam, and far in the future, a changed relationship with China. Ironically, the change in policy would be Nixon's initiative, not Kennedy's.

THE
SINO-SOVIET
SPLIT

American policy toward the People's Republic of China was based on Washington's assumption that Communist China was a puppet of the Soviet Union in an ideological monolith aimed at world domination. But Mao's victory in 1949 was the result of a lifetime's struggle which came only after many hardships and defeats, with little help from the Soviet Union. There is no doubt that Mao regarded his victory as his own accomplishment. Nationalism was as important to Mao as the Marxist-Leninist ideology, which he adapted to the indigenous conditions of China.

The establishment of the Chinese Communist Party (CCP) in 1921 was inspired by two events—the Russian Revolution of 1917 in which the Communists came to power, and the Chinese May 4th Movement of 1919. From the start, ideology was entangled with nationalism.

Even in the beginning, relations between the CCP and the Soviet Union were marked by some friction over Moscow's inclination to use the CCP for its own purposes. At Moscow's instruction, the CCP agreed in 1923 to the United Front with Sun's Kuomintang party. Many Chinese Communists were uncomfortable with this arrangement. They became more discontented after the death of Sun and the rise of Chiang.

Within the Kremlin there were also doubts about the Soviet policy toward China, and a "Who lost China?" debate ensued. After Lenin's death, Stalin and Leon Trotsky struggled for control of the Communist party in Russia. Trotsky asserted that the Chinese Communists should be creating "soviets," or local committees to encourage revolution, rather than cooperating with "reactionaries," the forces in power. When Chiang turned against the Communists in 1927, Trotsky's position seemed vindicated. Trotsky accused Stalin of being the "gravedigger of the Chinese revolution." Even with Stalin's ultimate victory for control of the Russian party, and Trotsky's subsequent exile, there was no change in Stalin's policy toward China. He could not afford to acknowledge that Trotsky had been right.

Stalin's continued support for Chiang's Kuomintang split the Communist party of China. After the massacre in Shanghai, the main body of Communists moved to the countryside, forming soviets among the peasants. The small "central committee" that remained in Shanghai, loyal to Moscow, was never again a real force in the CCP.

THE RISE OF MAO

Among the Communist Chinese organizing in the countryside were Mao Tse-tung and Chu Teh, who together began forming a Communist army. By 1931, the Communists were powerful enough to declare a Chinese Soviet Republic with Mao as chairman. Contact with the peasants led Mao to develop a new theory of guerrilla organization and warfare.

Mao saw that the classic Marxist doctrine that revolution had to spring from the proletariat, or working class, did not apply to China. In China the peasant farmers, rather than the industrial workers of the cities, would have to provide the main support for revolution.

Chiang's five extermination campaigns against the Communists in the countryside forced the Communists to develop a strong, coherent organization. On the Long March the Communists came into contact with the many national groups within China, giving Mao new insight into his country's problems. The enormous struggle to keep his forces together during the Long March, and his success against great odds, made Mao the undisputed leader of the CCP and a commanding presence throughout China.

During the Yenan period, Mao built a strong base. There is no evidence that he obtained active support from Moscow, which formally recognized the Kuomintang government. In 1938 Mao called for the "Sinification of Marxism," an indication he was not a docile follower of the "Party line" in Moscow.

Stalin himself underestimated the strength of Mao's forces. In conversation with U.S. presidential adviser Harry Hopkins in March 1945, Stalin spoke contemptuously of Mao, saying that the Nationalists had better leaders. He often referred to the CCP as "margarine Communists"—not as good as the real thing. Even after the war, Stalin did not shift his support to Mao, with the exception of some help and equipment in Manchuria. He kept his promise of recognition to the Nationalist regime.

Stalin made a rare admission to a Yugoslavian delegation shortly before Tito's break with Moscow in 1948. "It is true," Stalin said, "that we have also made mistakes. For example, after the war we invited the Chinese comrades to Moscow to discuss the situation in China with them. We told them frankly that we felt the prospects of a revolt in China were nil, and that the Chinese comrades should seek a *modus vivendi* with Chiang Kai-shek, take part in his government, and disband their army. The Chinese . . . went back to China and did something quite different. They assembled their forces, organized their army, and are now, as we see, in the process of defeating Chiang Kai-shek's troops. In the case of China . . . it turned out that the Chinese comrades were right and not the Soviets."

In July 1949, Mao proclaimed that his government would "lean to one side." In the world struggle between the two camps—the socialist led by the Soviet Union, and the capitalist led by the United States—China would side with the Soviet Union.

A SINO-SOVIET ALLIANCE

Mao went to Moscow in December 1949 and in February 1950, the two countries signed the thirty-year Treaty of Friendship, Alliance, and Mutual Assistance. They agreed that if either nation were attacked by Japan or "any state allied to it" (meaning the United States), the other would immediately give strong military backing to the extent of its capability. In a separate agreement the Chinese received economic backing in a five-year $300 million loan. Provisions for the return of Port Arthur, Dairen, and the Chinese Changchun Railway to full Chinese control were made. But the Chinese also had to make concessions to the Soviets: the Chinese surrendered their influence in Outer Mongolia and North Korea.

From 1950 until the death of Stalin in March 1953, the Sino-Soviet alliance appeared solid. The two countries were united as ideological partners in the Cold War in their opposition to the United States. The Soviet Union was clearly the dominant partner. China's economy was in shambles. Forty years of war, occupation, and revolution meant that the reconstruction task was enormous. The only source of foreign aid and technology for the reconstruction was the Soviet Union. In addition, the USSR would be a strong shield if the Communists were to take Formosa. During this period Stalin was extolled as a hero and the Soviet Union was emulated as a model for China.

But the tie between the two countries had tensions. Chinese nationalism chafed at the temporary Russian privileges in Manchuria and perhaps also at the role of junior partner. There was discontent with the small amount of economic aid offered by Russia. But with the American embargo on trade, China had no other alternatives.

The first test of the Sino-Soviet alliance came with the Korean War. After MacArthur's forces advanced to the Yalu, the Chinese bore the brunt of the fighting, although Stalin sent supplies for Mao's troops. Peking's alliance with Moscow, placing China under the Soviet nuclear umbrella, was one factor in deterring the United States from attacking Manchuria.

With Stalin's death in 1953, Sino-Soviet relations entered their most amicable phase. At Stalin's funeral, Chou En-lai was given a place of honor alongside the other Communist leaders. As a sign of new flexibility, four days after Stalin's death Chou put forth a new proposal in the Korean truce talks that was similar to one that the Communists had earlier rejected.

The new leaders of the Soviet Union, Nikolai Bulganin and Nikita Khrushchev, paid a visit to Peking in October 1954. The Soviet Union relinquished its "special position" on Chinese territory, offered increased economic assistance, and agreed to additional technical aid. There was talk of "two leaders" in the socialist camp.

China began to play a greater role in the world, particularly among the nations of Asia and Africa. The Bandung Conference of 1955 in Indonesia brought these "Third World" nations together to discuss mutual interests. Chou played a leading role in the conference. This was mutually advantageous to China and the USSR, as nonwhite nations of the world looked at Chinese achievements with admiration and saw that Communism could be successful in a non-European country.

The years 1954 to early 1957 also saw the Chinese Communists making overtures to the United States for normalization of relations. Chou suggested at the Bandung Conference that the Formosa question could be settled peacefully and attempts were made at establishing some contact between China and the United States.

EARLY SIGNS OF A SINO-SOVIET SPLIT

By 1957, there were signs of a rift between the Chinese and the Soviets. Khrushchev's de-Stalinization policies were not received favorably in Peking. The Chinese Communists had modeled many of their programs on Stalin's, and Mao's role in China was likened to that of Stalin's in Russia. There seems also to have been a personality conflict between Khrushchev and Mao.

In 1957, the Russian Sputnik, the first artificial satellite, was launched into space, and the Soviets developed an ICBM delivery system for nuclear warheads. In October, Russia agreed to share nuclear weapons with China. Mao felt the Soviet Union had overtaken the United States as a great power. Mao went to Moscow in November for the second and last time. Declaring "the east wind prevails over the west wind," Mao appeared to be pushing the Russians to use their weapons breakthrough to pursue a more aggressive anti-American policy. Earlier, Mao had harshly attacked the United States' "two-China intrigues." However, the Russians were now interested in improving relations with the United States, and were afraid that Mao's offensive posture would heighten international tensions.

The 1958 Formosa Strait crisis brought new strains to the Sino-Soviet alliance. The Chinese were disappointed in the level of Russian support for them at the beginning of the crisis. Although Khrushchev was to declare his willingness to defend China in case of American attack, Mao felt his support came too late and was too limited. The slowness of the Russians' response probably reflected their unwillingness to be dragged into a nuclear confrontation. As Chiang sought to involve the United States in its dispute with the People's Republic, so, too, did Mao look for more support from his Russian allies. Both Chiang and Mao were disappointed.

Mao's internal policy produced the "Great Leap Forward" of 1958. He announced a vast program of national communes that would realize the Marxist ideal of distributing to each according to need. Thus, Mao claimed, the communes represented an unprecedented achievement and a model for the rest of the world. Implicitly, the Chinese were claiming that they had overtaken the Russians on the road to a full Communist society.

The Russians publicly ignored the Chinese communes

and emphasized that a completely communistic state required a strong industrial base such as that in the Soviet Union. When reports during 1959–60 indicated that the Great Leap Forward had failed in its objectives, the Russians were smug.

In 1959 there was a further widening of the rift. The 21st Communist Party Congress in the Soviet Union declared that war between the capitalist and socialist states could be permanently avoided even if capitalism survived. The Russians soon acted on this important ideological repudiation of Lenin's doctrines. Soviet Deputy Premier Anastas Mikoyan visited the United States in January 1959 to pursue "peaceful coexistence" and prepare for a visit by Premier Khrushchev later in the year.

In June 1959, the Soviet Union formally rejected a Chinese request for a sample atomic bomb. And when fighting broke out in a border dispute between China and India, the Russians remained neutral. The Chinese portrayed the neutralist Russian stance as a betrayal of "proletarian internationalism."

In the fall, Khrushchev became the first Soviet leader to visit the United States, taking the softest line toward the West since World War II. Khrushchev and Eisenhower met at the presidential retreat, Camp David, where the Russian told the president that he would not give atomic weapons to the Chinese and seemed to agree to the permanent existence of two Chinas. In a widely reported remark made during his trip, Khrushchev confided to U.S. Senator Hubert Humphrey that the Chinese communes were tried in the Soviet Union and did not work. Khrushchev had made a similar slur against the Chinese policies on a trip to Poland in July. This was the first public criticism between the two countries.

The Chinese responded to Khrushchev with fury. They wanted the greatest possible pressure put on the United States all over the world, and charged America with using negotiation and relaxation of tension as a "smoke screen" to facilitate American "aggression" against national liberation movements in the underdeveloped world.

The National People's Congress of China repeated the claim that the United States had taken Formosa by force and that it was China's right to liberate it.

In the United States, reaction to the Sino-Soviet quarrel was subdued, as the extent of the rift was still not known. On October, 16, 1959, Assistant Secretary of State Andrew Berding named China as the greatest threat to world peace in light of the "improvement in the international atmosphere" created by the Camp David talks.

AN OPEN BREAK

In April 1960, the Sino-Soviet dispute became public. The Chinese Communist party directly attacked the Soviet position on peaceful coexistence on the grounds that it was weakening the socialist camp. The Chinese disputed the Russian "line" that nuclear weaponry necessitated a change in the Communist strategy of world revolution. They said that local wars would not necessarily lead to world war and that anticolonial wars of liberation should still be encouraged and not be sacrificed to the Russians' misguided notions of the need to appease the United States. The Russians responded in ideological discussions in party congresses, and in late summer of 1960 removed all their advisers and technicians from China.

China began new foreign policy offensives based on their now-cool relationship with the Soviets. In the summer of 1960 Chou offered a peace pact between China, the United States, and other Pacific powers to establish a "nonnuclear" zone in Asia and the Western Pacific. If the Chinese could not count on nuclear support from the USSR, they wanted to forestall the U.S. threat. The offer was characterized by U.S. State Department officer Lincoln White as a "propaganda gesture."

An important interview with Chou by longtime Chinese observer Edgar Snow appeared in *Look* magazine in January 1961. Chou said that the USSR and China differed on many matters but not on the feeling that war could be avoided. Although China supported Russia's proposals for international disarmament, Chou said, China was not bound by any disarmament agreement reached without its participation. He said relations between the United States and the People's Republic of China could improve if the U.S. protection was withdrawn from Taiwan.

Despite Chou's overtures to the United States, hostility between the People's Republic and the USSR increased. By 1962 the Chinese were calling on other socialists to revolt against the Soviet Communist party as betrayers of the revolution. The Chinese portrayed themselves as the true leaders of revolution in the Third World.

The Russians signed the Nuclear Test Ban Treaty in the summer of 1963; this sign of more peaceful relations between the United States and the USSR aroused Chinese anger. The Chinese used the expression "two-handed policy" to refer to the U.S. policy of extending the hand of friendship toward Russia while turning its fist to China. The Chinese began to speak of a "capitalist restoration" in the Soviet Union.

The idea that the United States might capitalize on the Sino-Soviet split was advanced hesitantly in the United States. By the middle 1960s the American people saw the Chinese as a greater enemy than the Soviets. A Gallup poll of 1967 showed 71 percent of Americans saw China as the greatest threat to peace, the USSR 20 percent, and the rest undecided.

With the forced retirement of Khrushchev in 1964, new Russian leadership tried to heal the schism with China. Ironically, the growing war in Vietnam remained an object of dispute in the Communist camp. In 1964 and 1965, the Soviets called for a reconvening of the Geneva Conference which had failed to unify Vietnam in 1954. The Chinese at first supported this move but then turned against the proposal. They accused the USSR of plotting with the United States to find a face-saving way out of Vietnam.

UPHEAVAL IN CHINA

In 1966, Mao launched the Great Proletarian Cultural Revolution. This massive upheaval in China came from the aging leader's belief that his nation was falling into the same kind of stolid bureaucracy that had caused Russia to lose its revolutionary fervor. The Russians were now denounced as "revisionists" and "bourgeois." Within China, similar "revisionists," or "capitalist roaders," were weeded out to ensure the permanently revolutionary character of the Chinese regime. Mao's handpicked successor, Liu Shao-chi, was labeled the "Chinese Khrushchev," and purged. At the same time, the Chinese Communist party severed formal relations with the Russian Communist party.

With its complete break with the Soviet Union, China faced the prospect of being an enemy of both the world superpowers. The Chinese abandoned the notion of a socialist camp. The socialist world, in the new Maoist view, was composed of countries that differed in their degree of revisionism. The Soviet Union had become a nation of "social imperialism." Those Chinese who had favored a rapprochement with the Soviet Union were demoted. The purge particularly affected high army officers.

Chinese policy was that both the Soviet Union and the United States shared the position of "principal enemy." The Chinese were convinced that the two were in collusion in a "holy alliance" against China. For a short time in the late 1960s the impression in the United States was that China had gone mad and was devouring itself.

As the Cultural Revolution began to fade, there were signs that the Soviet Union was emerging in Mao's thinking as the "principal enemy." In northeast China, Manchuria borders on the Soviet Union along the Ussuri River. In 1966 the Soviet Union began a major troop buildup on its side of the river. Small border skirmishes in the late 1960s escalated in 1969. The warfare produced sizable casualties on both sides. More than a million Soviet troops with modern offensive weapons were stationed on the border.

This unmistakable evidence of a Sino-Soviet split brought the United States to a new diplomatic effort to exploit its position as the third member of the triangular relationship.

THE VIETNAM WAR

Not only did the Korean War harden American policy toward the Chinese Communist regime, but it signaled the beginning of an American commitment to combat Communism actively throughout Asia. The largest commitment of American aid would eventually go to the conflict in Vietnam.

Since late 1946, Communist Vietminh rebels, with increasing amounts of aid from the Chinese Communists, had been fighting against French colonial rule of Indochina. The Truman administration believed that the Vietminh revolt was part of a Communist plan to increase Chinese influence in Asia. In May 1950, *The New York Times* reported that there was an agreement between China and the Vietminh leader, Ho Chi Minh, to provide aid to the Vietminh. Right after the outbreak of the Korean War, the United States began to subsidize the French effort, contributing in all about $3 billion in military aid.

The Eisenhower administration continued the Truman policies in Indochina, but the French position steadily weakened. Secretary of State Dulles, Vice-President Nixon, and some senior military advisers advocated American air strikes to aid the French. There was talk of using the atomic bomb to stop a Communist victory.

Facing the imminent defeat of their garrison at Dienbienphu, Vietnam, the French decided to withdraw from the war on the best terms possible. The Geneva Conference of 1954, attended by nineteen nations, was called to arrange peace terms. Dulles briefly attended the conference, where he publicly snubbed Chou En-lai by refusing to shake his proffered hand of greeting. The snub was long remembered by Chou, who alluded to it seventeen years later during the historic visit of Nixon's national security adviser, Henry Kissinger.

The Geneva Accords signed in July 1954 called for France to leave Indochina (Vietnam, Laos, and Cambodia), a temporary division of Vietnam at the 17th parallel to permit the disengagement of forces, and the creation of a unified nation after free elections in 1956. Although the United States refused to sign the accords, Dulles informally agreed that the United States would abide by the terms.

U.S. INVOLVEMENT BEGINS

In 1954, American military advisers and CIA undercover operatives arrived in the Vietnamese city of Saigon. They were hoping to create the framework for a non-Communist government that would replace the French administration. This pro-American regime would serve not only as a barrier to Chinese expansion, but would also act as a symbolic alternative to Communist regimes in underdeveloped Third World nations. South Vietnam was to be a showcase for American democracy.

The United States supported Ngo Dinh Diem, who, with extensive American military and economic aid, established himself in Saigon by the end of 1954. Instead of permitting the agreed-on countrywide elections, Diem proclaimed the Republic of Vietnam as an independent nation south of the 17th parallel. The United States immediately recognized Diem's regime and offered to protect its "independence and freedom." Eisenhower, in his memoirs, admitted that Ho

Chi Minh would have won the promised elections, so the United States aided Diem in blocking the election—in violation of the Geneva Accords. After 1956, the American position was that there were two independent nations of Vietnam.

In South Vietnam, an insurgent Communist force, the Viet Cong, began political and guerrilla operations against Diem's government. The North Vietnamese People's Republic of Vietnam sent aid to the Viet Cong. As the Viet Cong's influence increased, so did American aid to Diem. During Eisenhower's administration the aid was limited to economic assistance and the presence of military advisers, although the CIA contributed significant military support.

With the presidency of John F. Kennedy, American military aid to Diem became stronger. In 1956, Kennedy had described South Vietnam as the "cornerstone of the free world in Southeast Asia."

Although Kennedy s   need to improve relations with China, he purs   vative policies, and for his secretary of sta'   e Dean Rusk, known for his unswerving ho   to the Chinese Communists. At a news conference on   ebruary 6, 1961, Rusk affirmed the U.S. commitment to defend Taiwan. Those who opposed official recognition of Communist China still held to the hope that the People's Republic would collapse under continuing diplomatic isolation, and saw the policy as a means of expressing the U.S.'s disapproval of Mao's regime. The ban on travel and the trade boycott continued, but without the support of the U.S.'s allies.

Rumors during the first year of Kennedy's term that the United States might consider admitting Communist China to the UN brought a response from the U.S. Senate, which passed a resolution on July 28, 1961, opposing UN membership for or U.S. recognition of the People's Republic of China.

Like Eisenhower, Kennedy knew of the potency of the "Who lost China?" debate as a force in American politics. He was determined not to abandon Diem's regime in Saigon, although by 1962–63, Diem was losing areas of the South to Viet Cong control. During Kennedy's administration the number of American military advisers in South Vietnam increased from about 600 to 16,000.

The increase in American military advisers brought a warning from Peking on February 24, 1962, that the U.S. intervention was a "direct threat" to the security of China and the peace of Asia. Kennedy responded in a press conference on August 1, predicting that if the Chinese obtained nuclear weapons and continued with their policies it would be a "potentially more dangerous situation than [any] we faced since the end of the Second World War."

Kennedy's presidency was cut short by his assassination on November 22, 1963. On December 2, Chou En-lai called the assassination "a despicable, shameful act."

THE JOHNSON YEARS

Lyndon Johnson took office with a promise to continue the Kennedy policies. Yet in a December speech, Assistant Secretary of State for Far Eastern affairs Roger Hilsman declared that the United States should keep options open for negotiations with China when the Peking government abandoned its "venomous hatred of the U.S." Hilsman felt that the United States should broaden its contacts with Peking. The speech had been cleared with the White House, but it drew from Peking only the response that it was just a continuation of the "aggressive policy" of the United States. The tentative gesture toward Peking was not to be repeated until the United States had been dragged much deeper into the Vietnam morass.

Johnson stepped up American support for South Vietnam in 1964, and obliquely warned China on February 21 that "those engaged in external direction and supply" were engaged in a "deeply dangerous game."

American political leaders of both parties supported the effort to oppose a Communist victory in South Vietnam. Former Vice-President Nixon stated "a United States defeat in Vietnam means a Chinese Communist victory." Rusk, in a February 1964 speech, accused the Chinese of actively inciting the aggression in Vietnam.

In early August 1964, North Vietnamese torpedo boats were reported to have attacked two American destroyers in the Gulf of Tonkin, off North Vietnam, though in international waters. Johnson responded with American air strikes against North Vietnamese boats and naval bases. The House of Representatives passed without a dissenting vote the Gulf of Tonkin Resolution, authorizing Johnson to take all necessary steps to help nations in Southeast Asia that sought American assistance. The Senate passed the resolution by a vote of 88 to 2.

The Tonkin Gulf Resolution would later be used by Johnson as authorization to wage undeclared war in the area on a scale unimagined in 1964. But in the presidential elections that fall, Johnson's opponent was Senator Barry Goldwater, who urged the use of tactical nuclear weapons to repel aggression in Vietnam. Johnson, playing the role of a steady cold warrior who drew the line at risking nuclear war, won a lopsided victory.

Johnson's moderation gained appeal when the nightmare of U.S. policymakers came true: In October 1964, the People's Republic of China exploded its first atomic bomb. With the announcement of the successful test came a Chinese demand for an international conference to outlaw nuclear weapons and destroy existing stockpiles. The statement said, "China cannot remain idle and do nothing in the face of the ever-increasing threat posed by the United States. China is forced to conduct nuclear tests and develop nuclear weapons." In a televised speech, Johnson responded with a promise to support nonnuclear states if they were threatened with "nuclear blackmail."

In March 1964, the National Liberation Front, the political arm of the Viet Cong, appealed to the Chinese for military assistance. The Chinese responded that China was ready to send men "whenever the South Vietnamese people want them." From 1965 to 1968 the Chinese sent about 50,000 soldiers to Vietnam. They helped operate communications equipment and antiaircraft weapons but were never used in combat duty.

Beginning in June 1964, the United States began building air and naval bases in South Vietnam to aid the war effort. A Viet Cong raid on American barracks at Pleiku in February 1965 was answered by U.S. Air Force bombing raids on military targets in North Vietnam. These moves were sharply denounced by the Chinese. In a curt reference to the Korean War, they stated, ". . . you have been taught a lesson on this score. . . . Do you want to have the lesson repeated in Indochina?"

In March 1965, the United States sent two battalions of marines to Vietnam. From this beginning grew the eventual American commitment of half a million fighting men there.

Johnson explained his decision to escalate the war in 1965 to his biographer, Doris Kearns. He said: "If I left that war and let the Communists take over South Vietnam, then I would be seen as a coward and my nation would be seen as an appeaser. . . . And I knew that if we let Communist aggression succeed in taking over South Vietnam there would follow in this country an endless national debate—a mean and destructive debate—that would shatter my Presidency, kill my administration, and damage our democracy. I knew that Harry Truman and Dean Acheson had lost effectiveness from the day the Communists took over China. I believed that the loss of China had played a large role in the rise of Joe McCarthy. And I knew that all these problems, taken together, were chickenshit compared with what might happen if we lost Vietnam."

Washington used the threat of Chinese expansionism as justification for the increasing cost of the war. In a response to an appeal from seventeen nonaligned nations in April 1965 to start peace negotiations without preconditions, Johnson said that the North Vietnamese in Hanoi were being "urged on" by China, "a nation which is helping the forces of violence in almost every continent. The contest in Vietnam is part of a wider pattern of aggressive purposes." Johnson offered a billion-dollar program of U.S. aid for the economic rehabilitation of Southeast Asia, including North Vietnam, if North Vietnamese troops were withdrawn from the South. The North responded with a call for a halt in the bombing, which by now included civilian as well as military targets, and a demand that the United States remove all its troops from the South.

American aircraft flying bombing missions over Vietnam were sometimes shot down over China, bringing new threats from the Chinese to "the United States marauders who are now extending the flames of their aggressive war in Indochina and conducting constant military provocations against China."

In an executive order of April 24, 1965, Johnson designated Vietnam and the waters adjacent to it a combat zone. Peking took this to include China's territorial waters in the vicinity of Hsisha Island. The U.S. escalation of the war was regarded by China as a threat to its security. The danger of U.S. confrontation with a nuclear-armed China increased.

FULBRIGHT COMMITTEE HEARINGS

By 1966 domestic opposition to the war had grown and in March 1966, Senator William Fulbright announced that the Senate Foreign Relations Committee would hold hearings on U.S.–China relations as an educational experience for the American people and to lessen the dangers of war. Fulbright said, "Some of our military experts are confident that China will not enter the war in Vietnam; their confidence would be more reassuring if it did not bring to mind the predictions of military experts in 1950 that China would not enter the Korean War, as well as more recent predictions about an early victory in Vietnam."

The Fulbright Committee hearings opened on March 8, and provided the first chance for many Americans to hear what many students of China thought about the U.S.'s China policy. A. Doak Barnett of Columbia University urged that the United States change its policy toward China from one "of containment plus isolation to one of containment without isolation." This meant checking military aggression but seeking to involve the Chinese in the international community.

Many scholars echoed Barnett's advice. John K. Fairbank of Harvard University said the Chinese should participate in international conferences and be permitted membership in the UN "even if they said they would dynamite the place."

Two other Harvard professors, John H. Lindbeck and Benjamin J. Schwartz, agreed that China should be brought into normal participation in international affairs. Lindbeck said China was more preoccupied with internal development than with promoting revolutions around the world. Both Lindbeck and Schwartz cautioned that there would be danger of Chinese intervention if the Viet Cong and North Vietnam faced defeat.

The Fulbright Committee also heard testimony in support of current U.S. policy: George E. Taylor of the University of Washington said, "At the present time there is no advantage to the United States in talking about [Communist China's] recognition or admission to the UN and there are a great many disadvantages . . . Why help the Peking regime when it is in trouble?"

Still other experts testifying before the committee advised a middle course. Robert A. Scalapino of the University of California said the United States "must find a way of making peaceful coexistence the only conceivable path for the next generation of Chinese leaders." He said China should be offered inducements to moderation, including UN membership, recognition, and economic and cultural exchanges. But, Scalapino added, the United States should maintain its position that any attempt to change the status of Taiwan by force would be met with American force.

JOHNSON'S POLICY
TOWARD CHINA

The Johnson administration made gestures toward the establishment of a relationship with the People's Republic of China. On March 9, 1966, permission was granted for U.S.

scholars and writers to visit China. On March 25, Rusk said the United States had been trying to improve relations by proposing exchanges of "newsmen, doctors and scholars, and weather information," but said there had been little response from Peking. Rusk complained that the People's Republic still insisted on the surrender of Taiwan as a condition of improved relations with the United States, and added that the People's Republic had indicated that its entry into the UN required expulsion of Nationalist China from the international body.

The People's Republic did not in fact seem eager to take advantage of the American gestures. On March 29, the Communist party newspaper in Peking rejected the proposed exchange of scholars and newsmen and said improved relations with the United States were "out of the question" until the Seventh Fleet and American troops left the Taiwan Strait. In editorials during the month of April the Chinese Communist newspaper charged that the United States was planning full-scale war in Asia, and had built a "new crescent cordon" in the Asian and Pacific region. This cordon extended from Japan, the Philippines, Taiwan, and South Korea to South Vietnam, Thailand, Malaysia, and India.

Facing two superpowers that it regarded as enemies, China turned inward. The outbreak of the Cultural Revolution with the stories of young Red Guards seizing power from the established bureaucracy, army officers, and teachers perplexed Americans. China was virtually closed to the outside world as Mao sought a renewal of the revolutionary spirit. Rusk thought the Cultural Revolution might enable the United States to negotiate more favorably with the Vietnamese, but China continued to give aid to Ho Chi Minh and the Viet Cong, although the Russians gave more.

The summary, and defense, of the Kennedy-Johnson policy toward China was given by Secretary Rusk in testimony before the House Committee for Far Eastern Affairs on March 16, 1966, and made public April 17.

As Rusk outlined them, China's three main foreign policy

objectives were (1) to bring China on the world stage as a great power, (2) to gain dominance over Asia, and (3) to win leadership of the world Communist revolution. Chinese development of nuclear weapons and missile systems, according to Rusk, was intended to intimidate other Asian nations. Since the Korean War, Rusk said, "Peiping has moved only against weaker foes and has carefully avoided situations which might bring it face to face with the United States."

Rusk listed ten elements in the U.S. policy toward the People's Republic: (1) The United States must remain firm in its determination to help those nations that were victims of direct or indirect use by or threat of force from Peking. (2) The United States must continue to assist Asian countries in building broadly based, effective governments. (3) The United States must honor its commitments to Nationalist China. (4) The United States must prevent expulsion of Nationalist China from the UN. (5) The United States must continue efforts to assure the People's Republic that the United States does not intend to attack the mainland. (6) The United States must not assume that the hostility of today's relations were unending. (7) The United States must continue to enlarge the possibilities for unofficial contacts with Peking, such as mail delivery, exchange of publications, exchange of news reporters, scholars, and scientists, and even the Chinese purchase of U.S. grain. (8) The United States must keep open the diplomatic talks at Warsaw. (9) The United States must be prepared to discuss disarmament and nonproliferation of atomic weapons with the People's Republic. (10) The United States must continue to keep its own policies up-to-date by analyzing information on China. Rusk also expressed a hope of restoration of ties of friendship between mainland China and the United States.

The Vietnam War continued to produce incidents that brought angry rhetoric to the U.S.–China relationship. On June 17, 1967, China detonated its first hydrogen bomb. From that point its perceived threat to world stability necessitated a change in U.S. policy.

Such a change was not to come during Johnson's administration. The Vietnam War had wrecked his presidency, just as he feared withdrawal would have. Facing a country torn by dissension and protest, Johnson declared on March 31, 1968, that he would not seek reelection.

In the face of military advice that it would be necessary to escalate the war still further in order to win it, Johnson stopped the bombing and began the winding down of the war. With the new year a new president would begin to disengage U.S. troops from Vietnam and shape a new China policy.

THE OPENING
OF RELATIONS

Richard Nixon's election in 1968 seemed to offer little chance of a shift in the basic U.S. policy toward China. He was thought of as a cold warrior par excellence, having been prominent among those in the 1950s who demanded to know "Who lost China?" Even before the United States entered the Vietnam conflict, Nixon had urged stronger American action in the area, believing that the Chinese had to be contained in Southeast Asia.

The only indication that Nixon might be more flexible than preceding presidents in his China policy was an article that he wrote for *Foreign Affairs* in 1967. Called "Asia After Vietnam," Nixon's article advocated even greater efforts to contain China militarily and reaffirmed Nixon's opposition to the admission of Communist China to the UN and American diplomatic recognition. Yet he also argued that American policy should attempt to persuade the People's Republic to change its "imperialistic ambitions." By implication, a change in Chinese policy would bring an American response.

MOVES TOWARD U.S.–
CHINA RELATIONS

After Nixon's election, the Communist Chinese proposed a February 20 meeting to resume the long-stalled Warsaw talks between the two nations. In addition, the Chinese called on the United States to agree on the five principles of peaceful coexistence: mutual respect for territorial integrity and sovereignty, mutual nonaggression, mutual noninterference in internal affairs, equality and mutual benefit, and peaceful coexistence. These five points would later become part of the joint Shanghai Communiqué between Nixon and Chou.

At Nixon's first news conference as president-elect, he noted the Chinese offer and said he looked forward to the February talks in Warsaw. But he reaffirmed his opposition to the admission of Communist China to the UN.

In his inaugural address, Nixon extended a surprisingly open hand. He declared: "After a period of confrontation, we are entering an era of negotiation. Let all nations know that during this administration our lines of communication will be open. We seek an open world—open to ideas, open to the exchange of goods and people, a world in which no people, great or small, will live in angry isolation. We cannot expect to make everyone our friend, but we can try to make no one our enemy." In February 1969, Nixon ordered a comprehensive National Security Council study of U.S.–China policy.

The events of March 1969 gave a bit of momentum to the U.S. move toward China. Senator Edward Kennedy made a major speech critical of the U.S.'s assumptions in its China policy. He called for a new policy based on the realization that the policy of isolation and containment had not worked.

Kennedy advocated discussing the establishment of full diplomatic relations with the People's Republic of China, removing American forces from Taiwan, and making clear the U.S. desire for a peaceful resolution of Taiwan's status. He also proposed that the United States remove its opposition to Communist China's admission to the UN.

The other major event of March was the fighting in the Ussuri River region over Chenpao Island between the Soviet Union and China. The fighting was major in scope, involving thousands of troops, tanks, and artillery, with heavy casualties on both sides. Unlike other Sino-Soviet clashes, the news of this one became public. Throughout 1969 it was rumored that the Soviets were planning a nuclear strike against China. The reports exploded the notion of a monolithic Communist world.

China was still emerging from the period of Cultural Revolution, during which the Soviets were castigated as "social imperialists." In China, the number one enemy was now regarded as the USSR. But the Chinese were still seeking to determine the intentions of the Nixon administration.

Nixon and his national security adviser, Henry Kissinger, realized that the Vietnam conflict and the Sino-Soviet split provided an opportunity for a different China policy. An accommodation with the People's Republic could allow Washington to play off the Soviets and Chinese against each other, and obtain Soviet concessions on arms limitation. The Chinese might be induced to bring pressure on North Vietnam to agree to peace terms acceptable to the United States.

Nixon's policies toward the Vietnam conflict tended to ease Chinese fears. On May 14, the U.S. president issued an eight-point peace formula calling for mutual withdrawal of forces. Nixon's proposal included the Vietnamization of the forces in the South—the United States would continue to support South Vietnam, but gradually withdraw its own troops. On June 8, Nixon announced the "immediate" withdrawal of 25,000 Americans.

In a July statement which was later to be known as the Nixon Doctrine, the president asserted that the United States would not become involved in more wars like Vietnam. Although the United States would keep its treaty commitments, Nixon said, it would furnish only military and economic assistance that was ". . . appropriate. But we shall look to the nation directly threatened to assume the primary responsibility of providing the manpower for its defense." Nixon's actions in removing troops and his statements about future commitment of forces did much to quell Chinese fears of a military confrontation with the United States.

In seeking to disengage from Vietnam, both Nixon and Kissinger were concerned with securing a "decent interval" between the removal of American troops and the time when the South Vietnamese would have to come to terms with the North. To do this, the South would have to be strengthened sufficiently to defend itself. Nixon used this objective as a rationale for expanding the war into Cambodia, where Communist troops had established bases.

The Cambodian "incursion" in 1970 outraged the Chinese, who backed the former Cambodian ruler Norodom Sihanouk, toppled in a 1969 coup by Lon Nol, who acceded to the American incursion. The event was personally denounced by Mao, who called on the world to unite "and defeat the U.S. aggressors and all their running dogs." Even so, the United States continued its troop withdrawal from Vietnam.

In July 1969 the Nixon administration had announced a relaxation of restrictions on American travel in China. Passports specially validated for China would be issued to scholars, students, doctors, and scientists. In January 1970, the Chinese suggested a resumption of the Warsaw talks, which had been suspended again after the Cambodian coup in the preceding March.

Throughout 1970, a serious power struggle took place in China between Mao and Lin Piao, Mao's heir apparent. Lin Piao was apparently opposed to any form of compromise with the United States. He pointed out the continuing American support for Taiwan. But Mao won out with his argument that China could not deter an attack from the Soviet Union if it were engaged in active hostilities with the United States. News of this "debate" filtered out slowly. One indication of its result came in an interview Mao gave Edgar Snow in December 1970. According to Snow, "Mao would be happy to talk with him [Nixon], either as a tourist or as President."

Nixon was sending comparable signals of reconciliation. In March 1970, the State Department announced that U.S. passports would be validated for mainland China for any legitimate purpose, and in April the licensing of non-strategic American goods for export to China was authorized. In October 1970, on a visit to Romania, Nixon used the official name for the Chinese government: the People's Republic of China. This was the first time an American president had used the term.

In his State of the Union address to Congress on February 25, 1971, Nixon made a clear offer. He said, "In this decade, therefore, there will be no more important challenge than that of drawing the People's Republic of China into a constructive relationship with the world community. . . . We are prepared to establish a dialogue with Peking." He added: "In the coming year I will carefully examine what further steps we might take to create broader opportunities for contacts between the Chinese and American peoples, and how we might remove needless obstacles to the realization of these opportunities." On March 15, the United States ended all passport restrictions on American travel to China.

"PING-PONG DIPLOMACY"

These actions brought an unusual response from the Chinese. On April 6, 1971, the Chinese extended an invitation to the U.S. table-tennis team that was then visiting Japan. The offer was accepted, and Peking issued visas to seven Western journalists to cover the visit. Chou received the American team in Peking, stating, "With your acceptance of our invitation, you have opened a new page in the relations of the Chinese and American people." This was no exaggeration, for the extensive television coverage in the United States broke the information blockade on China.

On April 20, the United States announced that the People's Republic had accepted a reciprocal invitation to send a Ping-Pong team to the United States. The same day, Nixon ordered a relaxation of the trade embargo with China. This "Ping-Pong diplomacy" brought a favorable response from the American people. A Gallup poll on May 30 revealed that 45 percent of Americans favored the admission of Red China to the UN; 38 percent were opposed.

In conducting an opening to China, Nixon was in a secure position because of his strong anti-Communist credentials. It was unlikely that he could be effectively criticized as being "soft on Communism." Popular support for his policy encouraged him to take further steps.

But the sticking point in improving relations with the People's Republic remained the American commitment to Taiwan. The United States had formally agreed that the Taiwan government represented all of China. A presidential commission began to investigate the possibility of admitting Peking to the UN without excluding Taiwan. The commission reported: "This is not a question of dual representation for one China but the provision of two seats for two governments." If this was an American probe to see if Red China's opposition to Taiwan had softened, it failed. On May 4, Peking denounced the statement as "brazen interference."

Communist China's two principal enemies also criticized the Nixon initiatives. Chiang Kai-shek, in a television interview, said, "Such [People's Republic] tactics of external infiltration and subversion have borne their first fruit. . . ."

The Soviets added their voice in opposition. On May 5, the USSR accused the Nixon administration of pursuing an "anti-Soviet objective."

Soon, however, there was an influx of American visitors to the mainland. The most important one was Nixon's adviser, Henry Kissinger. Feigning illness while on a trip to Pakistan so that reporters would not notice his absence, Kissinger secretly flew to Peking in July 1971 for conversations with Chou En-lai.

The most important point of difference was Taiwan. Chou sought an American acknowledgment that there was only one China and that Taiwan was part of it. Kissinger refused any abandonment of the U.S.'s longtime ally, but said that the United States would be happy to have an intermediate form of recognition. The U.S. military relationships with the

Philippines, Japan, and South Korea were no longer problems, for by now the People's Republic was glad to have an American military presence in Asia as a barrier to the Soviet Union. On July 10, Chou invited Nixon to visit China.

THE NIXON VISIT

Five days later, Nixon announced his decision to go to the People's Republic of China "to seek the normalization of relations between the two countries and to exchange views on questions of concern to the two sides." Nixon added, "Our action in seeking a new relationship with the People's Republic of China will not be at the expense of our old friends."

With the exception of some right-wing Republicans such as Senator James Buckley, and Senator John Tower, American response was favorable to the announcement.

In Peking the disclosure of the forthcoming visit was subdued. The *Peking People's Daily* of July, 16, 1971, carried the news in a small box on the lower-right-hand corner of the first page. President Nixon was to visit Peking to discuss "normalization of relations between the two countries" and there would be "an exchange of opinion on problems to both sides." The headline stories that day were about the visit of a Chinese delegation to North Korea.

Nationalist China was shocked and dismayed. Ambassador James C. H. Shen protested to the State Department the "shabby deal" his government was getting.

In August, the United States announced it was ending its opposition to the admission of the People's Republic to the UN, but repeated its opposition to the expulsion of Taiwan. But the United States was not able to control the genie it had released from the bottle. In spite of the frantic efforts of Secretary of State William Rogers to forge a two-China agreement to salvage Taiwan's seat, the General Assembly of the UN passed a resolution to seat the People's Republic of China as the sole Chinese representative in the UN. Taiwan was expelled. During this time, Kissinger was back in Peking settling preparations for the Nixon visit.

President Richard Nixon conferred with Mao Tse-tung during his historic trip to Peking in 1972. Henry Kissinger is seated at the right.

President Nixon and his wife, accompanied by American media representatives, visited China during the week of February 21–28, 1972. The visit became a media event of the highest order. A new communications satellite, Intelstar 4, went into operation to cover the Nixon trip.

The Chinese response, controlled by the government, was calmer. Nixon was greeted at the airport by Chou and several other Chinese dignitaries. There were no crowds. Later that day, Nixon and Mao met for "frank and serious discussion." In the next seven days Nixon had several talks with Chinese leaders and did a great deal of sight-seeing, with the American press and TV cameras recording every possible moment.

On February 27, Chou and Nixon issued a joint statement subsequently called the Shanghai Communiqué. The communiqué was to be the basis of the subsequent negotiations toward normalization of relations. It was divided into five parts. The first was a general account of the president's visit to China. The second contained the two governments' differing views on Asian policy issues. China backed the Viet Cong peace proposal for Vietnam, and the United States repeated Nixon's earlier eight-point peace proposal. Other differences were expressed on Japan, Korea, and the India-Pakistan dispute.

The third section of the communiqué contained general rules of international relations to which both China and the United States subscribed. These included the five principles of peaceful coexistence that Chou had first enunciated at the Bandung Conference in 1955. This section also stated that "Both sides are of the view that it would be against the interests of the peoples of the world for any major country to collude with another against other countries, or for major countries to divide up the world into spheres of interest." This assurance was meant to placate the Soviet Union by assuring it that the United States and China were not uniting against it.

The fourth section dealt with the status of Taiwan. The Chinese stated: "The Taiwan question is the crucial question obstructing the normalization of relations between China and the United States; the Government of the People's Republic of China is the sole legal government of China; Taiwan is a province of China which has long been returned to the motherland; the liberation of Taiwan is China's internal affair in which no other country has the right to interfere; and all U.S. forces and military installations must be withdrawn from Taiwan. The Chinese Government firmly opposes any activities which aim at the creation of 'one China, one Taiwan,' 'one China, two governments,' 'two Chinas,' an 'independent Taiwan' or advocate that 'the status of Taiwan remains to be determined.' "

The United States declared: "The United States acknowledges that all Chinese on either side of the Taiwan Strait maintain there is but one China and that Taiwan is a part of China. The United States Government does not challenge that position. It reaffirms its interest in a peaceful settlement of the Taiwan question by the Chinese themselves. With this prospect in mind, it affirms the ultimate objective of the withdrawal of all U.S. forces and military installations from Taiwan. In the meantime, it will progressively reduce its forces and military installations on Taiwan as the tension in the area diminishes."

The fifth section stated that both sides agreed on the desirability of broadening "understanding between the two peoples." Both sides promised to promote contacts that would be mutually beneficial, "in such fields as science, technology, culture, sports, and journalism." In addition, "Both sides view bilateral trade as another area from which mutual benefit can be derived," and "agree to facilitate the progressive development of trade between their two countries."

Summing up and looking to the future, "The two sides expressed the hope that the gains achieved during this visit would open up new prospects for the relations between the two countries. They believe that the normalization of relations between the two countries is not only in the interest of the Chinese and American peoples but also contributes to the relaxation of tension in Asia and the world."

On his return to the United States, Nixon received general acclaim. In a nationally televised talk, he said that the trip had shown that "nations with very deep and fundamental differences can learn to discuss those differences calmly, rationally, and frankly without compromising principles," and that this discussion was "the basis for a structure of peace."

Not surprisingly the Nationalist Chinese foreign ministry and the Taiwan newspapers denounced the communiqué. The Nationalist foreign ministry said that the question of Taiwan could be solved "only when the government of the

Republic of China [Taiwan], the sole legitimate government elected by all people of China, had succeeded in its task of the recovery of the unification of China and the deliverance of our compatriots. There is definitely no other alternative." A Taiwanese newspaper commented that Nixon had "gained nothing in return for his statement about the withdrawal. Not even a specific commitment that the Chinese Communists will not resort to the use of force in the Taiwan area."

OBSTACLES TO NORMALIZATION

Despite the success of the Nixon visit, there would be a long road to full normalization of relations. American troops stayed in Taiwan and the Vietnam War dragged on. In May 1972, the United States mined North Vietnamese ports, an action described in the Chinese press as a "dangerous move." Yet the compromise agreement held: Nixon felt that with the ending of the Vietnam War and the consequent lowering of tensions in Asia, it would be feasible to begin the American troop withdrawal from Taiwan.

Nixon's visit was not a campaign issue in the presidential elections of 1972. Both Democrats and Republicans approved it. The Democratic party platform called for the United States to take concrete steps necessary to establish regular diplomatic relations.

After an overwhelming victory over Democratic Senator George McGovern in the election of 1972, Nixon took further steps toward normalization of relations with the People's Republic. The long-hoped-for Vietnam cease-fire was signed in Paris on January 27, 1973, and Nixon withdrew the remaining U.S. troops from Vietnam. The establishment of liaison officers in Peking and Washington indicated that the U.S.–China détente was gaining momentum. Trade between the two nations soon increased. But, the momentum toward normalization broke down because of domestic political events in the United States. By the middle of 1973, the Nixon administration was mired in the Watergate scandals. Nixon's struggle to extricate himself paralyzed the administration.

By 1974, now fighting desperately to avoid impeachment, Nixon needed the support of right-wing Republicans who were among his last supporters. The People's Republic continued to demand a break with Taiwan as the price of full diplomatic relations. Nixon could not afford to repudiate the U.S.–Taiwan mutual defense treaty, a move that would alienate the right wing of his party.

Nixon failed to save his presidency, and he resigned on August 9, 1974. His successor, Gerald R. Ford, was unable to prevent the fall of non-Communist governments in South Vietnam, Cambodia, and Laos in 1975. The shock to the United States brought a halt to the process of normalization of relations between the United States and China. In the grim atmosphere of defeat that permeated the United States, further concessions to the Chinese were impossible.

President Ford's visit to China in December 1975 accomplished little. In the months preceding the trip, a congressional resolution was put forward, though not passed, that expressed the mood of the country. The resolution demanded that nothing be negotiated that compromised the freedom of Taiwan.

Despite the death of Chiang Kai-shek in 1975, Taiwan continued its policy of claiming sovereignty over all of China. American troop levels on the island actually increased, and in 1976 American F-4 squadrons were sent to Taiwan, although later withdrawn. American economic ties to Taiwan also increased, and the Nationalists were permitted to open new consulates in the United States. The mutual defense treaty was still in force.

To the People's Republic leaders, the Americans seemed to be dragging their feet on the road to full normalization. Furthermore, the Ford-Kissinger attempts at détente with the Soviet Union, including the U.S.–Soviet Strategic Arms Limitation Treaty talks, aroused new Chinese suspicions.

Perhaps to give a sign of disappointment in the Ford polcies, the mainland Chinese invited former President Nixon to visit Peking early in 1976. The Chinese misjudged his influence in American politics if they felt his visit might help to moderate the opposition in the United States toward breaking relations with Taiwan. Nixon's report to President Ford on his second visit was never made public.

The deaths of Chou En-lai, Chu Teh, and Mao Tse-tung in 1976 swept away the old leadership of the Chinese Communist regime. In both the People's Republic of China and the United States, comparatively unknown figures would rise to power by the beginning of 1977. No one at the time could accurately predict what effect the new leadership would have on U.S.–China relations.

FULL RELATIONS

Before his death, Chou En-lai was concerned with trying to arrange a line of succession which would make the rapprochement with the West and increasing moderation possible. In 1973, he restored to leadership Deng Xiaoping, who had been purged in 1967 during the Cultural Revolution and denounced as a "capitalist roader." Deng was known for his pragmatic, nondoctrinaire approach to Chinese policy.

After Chou's death in January 1976, Mao nominated the previously obscure Hua Guofeng as Chou's successor as premier and Deng was once more removed from office a few months later.

With Mao's death in September, concern arose as to who would take his place as chairman of the Chinese Communist party. The dissension and chaos that had arisen during the Cultural Revolution made it unlikely that any single leader would be acceptable to all.

The answer was quick in coming. In October, Hua boldly ordered the arrest of a group of radicals who would later be denounced as the "Gang of Four." Best known was Mao's widow, Chiang Ching, who had led the most extreme efforts to rid China of any antirevolutionary influences.

NEW LEADERSHIP IN
CHINA AND THE U.S.

Hua's new leadership seemed anxious to promote pragmatic programs, and many officials who had been disgraced during the Cultural Revolution were soon restored to positions of authority. The most prominent was Deng, who in the summer of 1977 became vice-premier. He began to use his renewed influence to speed China's modernization program.

In the United States, former Georgia Governor Jimmy Carter became president in 1977. The Carter administration put the full normalization of relations with China in the background of foreign policy concerns. The new administration's main concern was with relations with the Soviet Union. But after Secretary of State Cyrus Vance returned from a trip to Moscow in April 1977, during which the Soviets had rejected Carter's disarmament proposals, interest in normalization with China reawakened.

There remained, however, the problem of the Republic of China (Taiwan) and the termination of the 1955 U.S.–Taiwan mutual defense treaty. Such a termination, with one year's notice, had been provided for in the treaty, but acting on this clause, it was feared, might harm America's relations with other small countries allied to it.

Nor could the United States control the reaction of the Taiwan government, now led by Chiang's son and still rhetorically devoted to the goal of reclaiming the mainland, however remote a possibility that might seem. Taiwan could declare its independence as a separate nation, making it difficult for the United States to back the People's Republic's claims on it as part of China. Taiwan might repeat the People's Republic's switch and turn to the USSR for support. There were vague suggestions that Taiwan could be given "neutral" status, or a status similar to Hong Kong, which was tolerated by the Chinese as a British-controlled trading port, even though "officially" claimed by China. None of these solutions conformed to the U.S. commitment in the Shanghai Communiqué, which recognized only one China.

CARTER'S MOVE
TOWARD NORMALIZATION

In May 1977, Carter gave a major foreign policy address at the University of Notre Dame. He said, "We see the American-Chinese relationship as a central element in our global policy, and China as a key force for global peace."

In August 1977, Senator Edward Kennedy called for a break in diplomatic relations with Taiwan in order to pave the way for full normalization of relations with the People's Republic.

A small group of specialists in the State Department were assigned to explore U.S. options on China. Also in August, Secretary of State Cyrus Vance went to Peking on an "exploratory mission." He asked for the reversal of the present status, with liaison offices in Taiwan and formal diplomatic relations with Peking.

Vance also asked for an explicit promise by the Communist Chinese government that it would not use force in the unification of China, or the "liberation" of Taiwan. Deng rejected this request. Perhaps his influence and control were still shaky; in any event, he was unwilling to compromise on such an emotional issue.

Soon after Vance returned from his trip, the State Department secretly set up a group to draft legislation for preserving economic ties, trade, and cultural relationships with Taiwan after a U.S. recognition of the Peking government. The United States and Taiwan were bound by about sixty treaties and executive agreements covering tariff privileges, fishing, loans, and airline accords. The reason for the secrecy was that at this time the Carter administration was trying to get the Panama Canal Treaty through Congress and could not risk alienating a single member of the Senate. Ironically, it can be said that the Taiwan regime was saved by Panama in 1977, just as it had been by Hanoi in 1975 and by Korea in 1950.

In 1978, Deng began to consolidate his power in China, while maintaining his official position as deputy premier. His policies were strongly anti-Soviet; domestically, he continued his earlier efforts to modernize the nation's industry.

The Chinese also began to establish friendly relations with the Association of Southeast Asian Nations (ASEAN) —Indonesia, Malaysia, Thailand, Singapore, and the Philippines—all of whom had booming economies and anti-Communist governments. The major success of the Soviet Union in Southeast Asia was Vietnam, which had signed a Treaty of Peace and Friendship with the USSR.

U.S. policymakers had justified the enormous effort to save South Vietnam with the "domino theory," which predicted the fall of a succession of anti-Communist governments in Asia if South Vietnam went Communist. Ironically, the postwar period saw a heightening of tensions between Communist-led governments in the area. Border incidents between China, Vietnam, and Cambodia brought China into conflict with its southern neighbors. Nor did the ASEAN nations, presumably the most likely dominoes, seem to fear trade and recognition with the Chinese.

In May 1978, Carter sent his national security adviser, Zbigniew Brzezinski, to Peking to emphasize the Carter administration's commitment to normalizing relations, to urge greater Sino-American economic, scientific, and cultural cooperation if an accord on diplomatic recognition could not be reached. He also briefed the Chinese on the U.S.'s overall foreign policy, particularly the status of negotiations with the Soviets on arms control. The Chinese agreed to bilateral exchanges despite the lack of normalization.

Also in May, the Chinese invited the surviving members of the Dixie Mission and their families to visit Yenan, where Mao had first extended his offer of friendship more than thirty years before. After friendly toasts a Chinese spokesman noted that although his government believed Washington would eventually establish normal relations, Peking "could not wait forever."

The crucial point, on which the People's Republic refused to compromise, was that the United States sever diplomatic relations with Taiwan. For the United States such a move would abrogate a treaty with an ally, and cause disquiet and distrust among the U.S.'s other alliances. The United States had other reasons for its concern over Taiwan. The island occupies a key position in the Pacific East Asia security system, lies along shipping lanes to Korea and Japan, and is an example of a successful developing free economy in East Asia. Taiwan's per capita income was $250 in 1965 when U.S. economic aid came to an end; by 1978, the per capita income was $1400, with a fairly equal distribution among the inhabitants. The Kuomintang had gradually allowed broader popular participation in the government. In 1978, Taiwan was the U.S.'s eighth largest recipient of overseas exports.

ESTABLISHMENT OF
FULL RELATIONS

But in 1978 Carter made the decision that full relations with the People's Republic were more important than the commitment to Taiwan. In August, the president expressed hope for full diplomatic relations with the People's Republic, and talks toward recognition soon opened.

Carter's negotiators offered three main conditions. First was that normalization was contingent on continuing U.S. arms sales to Taiwan. Second was that recognition would be rescinded if Peking publicly contradicted public statements by American officials on their hope for a peaceful settlement of the Taiwan question. Third, Peking had to accede to some form of unofficial U.S. representation on the island of Taiwan.

Carter personally entered the China negotiations in September. He invited Ambassador Chai Zemin to the White House, where Carter stressed the need for some Chinese concessions.

There was a silence for six weeks, while discussions went on in Peking. Then on November 4, there was a breakthrough at the U.S.–Chinese talks in China. During this session, U.S. representative Leonard Woodcock gave Chinese Foreign Minister Huang Hua a draft of a communiqué announcing full relations, setting for the first time a target date of January 1, 1979. Huang requested clarification on some of the U.S. demands.

Four weeks went by without another response. But in that interval, three statements by Deng to reporters signaled Peking's willingness to proceed. He made it plain that Peking would not disrupt Taiwan's economic and political system.

On December 4, Woodcock was shown a Chinese draft of the proposed communiqué and was invited to meet with Deng to put the finishing touches on the joint statement. On December 12, Deng received Woodcock and agreed to the U.S. proposal, with reservations on arms sales to Taiwan. Deng assured Woodcock there would be no public Chinese contradiction of President Carter's statement of concern for a peaceful settlement of the Taiwan question.

The details of these negotiations had been secret, and so President Carter's announcement on December 15 that the United States had agreed to establish normal diplomatic relations with the People's Republic of China came as a surprise to the world. Taiwan's President Chiang Ching-kuo had been notified of the decision only hours earlier.

Reading from a joint communiqué, Carter announced to the country that "The United States of America and the People's Republic of China have agreed to recognize each other and to establish diplomatic relations as of January 1, 1979." On that date, the United States would also end diplomatic relations with Taiwan and give notice of its intention to abrogate the mutual defense treaty. The one-year notice would become effective in January 1980. All American forces would be withdrawn from Taiwan during the first four months of 1979.

The United States would still keep up trade and cultural relations with Taiwan, and would continue to sell arms to Taiwan, even after termination of the treaty. According to the statement, it was expected that the Taiwan issue would be "settled peacefully by the Chinese themselves."

The People's Republic of China statement read, in part:

Deng Xiaoping greets former President Richard Nixon at a White House dinner given in honor of the Chinese vice-premier in 1979. President Jimmy Carter looks on.

"As is known to all, the Government of the People's Republic of China is the sole legal Government of China and Taiwan is a part of China. The question of Taiwan was the crucial issue obstructing the normalization of relations between China and the United States. It has now been resolved . . . in the spirit of the Shanghai Communiqué. . . .

"As for the way of bringing Taiwan back to the embrace of the motherland and reunifying the country, it is entirely China's internal affair."

The Nationalist government on Taiwan issued its own statement, which read, in part: "The United States, by extending diplomatic recognition to the Chinese Communist regime, which owes its very existence to terror and suppression, is not in conformity with its professed position of safeguarding human rights and strengthening the capability of democratic nations to resist the totalitarian dictatorship. . . .

". . . the Republic of China shall neither negotiate with the Communist Chinese regime, nor compromise with Communism, and it shall never give up its sacred task of recovering the mainland and delivering the compatriots there."

Considering the intense emotion that the Chinese issue had prompted in American politics over the preceding thirty years, the reaction of the American public was surprisingly restrained. Although Senator Goldwater condemned the decision as a "cowardly act" that "stabs in the back the nation of Taiwan," most reaction was approving. Goldwater and a number of other senators introduced a court suit challenging the president's right to terminate a defense treaty without Senate approval. Among Goldwater's backers were some who favored normalization but felt that the decision should have been subject to Senate approval, as had the original treaty.

In December 1979, the Supreme Court refused to hear the case, effectively defeating the suit. Four of the justices said the issue was a "political question" that should not be considered by the high court. Three others concurred for other reasons in the decision not to hear arguments in the case.

Carter's announcement came after congressional elections for the year. The majority of Americans seemed to think that normalization would enhance the American strategic position in the world. A January 1979 Gallup poll found 58 percent approval for recognition of mainland China; 24 percent disapproved. However, 47 percent were opposed to derecognition of Taiwan; 35 percent approved.

American firms sent delegations to China seeking trade with the largest nation in the world, and even *Time* magazine made Deng Xiaoping its "Man of the Year," the first Chinese selected since Chiang himself forty years earlier.

Reaction in the two other countries most affected was predictable. Anti-American riots broke out on Taiwan, possibly induced by the government. Soviet President Leonid Brezhnev issued a warning: "The Soviet Union will most clearly follow what the development of American-Chinese relations will be in practice, and from this will draw appropriate conclusions for Soviet policy." Part of Carter's desire for an opening to China was to wring concessions from the Soviets on the SALT II talks then in progress.

RESULTS OF THE NEW RELATIONSHIP

Carter had also announced the impending visit to the United States of Chinese Vice-Premier Deng. The Chinese leader arrived for a nine-day visit on January 28, 1979. As the first Chinese Communist leader to enter the United States, he and his tour were subjected to widespread publicity and reawoke the curiosity of the American people about life in China. In China a television satellite hookup gave the Chinese people their first view of American life and its material accomplishments.

Amidst the hoopla Deng struck a strong anti-Soviet stance. His tour was marked by many public statements hailing the resumption of diplomatic relations and denouncing the threat of Soviet hegemony (predominant influence). "Hegemony," by now a buzz word to the Soviets meaning anti-Soviet policy in Asia, appeared in a joint Sino-American statement at the end of Deng's visit.

A group of Taiwanese gathered in Plains, Georgia, in December 1978, to protest the president's decision to recognize the People's Republic of China.

Soon after Deng's return to Peking, China launched an invasion to the south, intended to "punish" Vietnam. The Chinese and the Vietnamese had been feuding for the past two years, and Vietnam's invasion of Cambodia, whose government was backed by China, was sufficient motivation for the Chinese miltary action. In addition China cited Vietnam's cruel treatment of ethnic Chinese living in Vietnam. The timing of the attack made it appear China was taking the step with the approval of the United States.

The invasion produced disapproval in the United States. Officially, the government called for the Chinese to end their invasion, a stance prompted by fears that the Soviets would be drawn into the conflict. Nonetheless American disapproval was offset by the visit of U.S. Treasury Secretary W. Michael Blumenthal to Peking to discuss economic cooperation, while the Chinese were still in Vietnam.

The Chinese army proved to be less effective than expected, and the invasion did not force Vietnam to remove its troops from Cambodia. By April peace talks were under way.

Also in April the Chinese announced that they would not renew the 1950 Treaty of Friendship, Alliance, and Mutual Assistance with the Soviet Union. The Chinese seemed to have chosen a new ally among the world's superpowers, further confusing those who still thought in terms of a world struggle between Communism and capitalism.

Future relations between the United States and Taiwan were defined early in 1979 by congressional passage of the Taiwan Relations Act. The act expressed American "concern" over the future of Taiwan, and said that efforts to change Taiwan's status by other-than-peaceful means "including boycotts or embargoes," will be considered "a threat to the peace and security of the Western Pacific area and of grave concern to the United States." The act guaranteed the supply of defensive weapons to Taiwan, and maintained the right of the United States to resist the use of force against the people of Taiwan.

Although President Carter had stated the United States wanted to pursue an "evenhanded" policy toward the

USSR and the People's Republic of China, the deterioration of relations with the Soviet Union made such a policy difficult. Within Carter's own administration there was a split. Vance was strongly committed to a strategy of equilibrium to prevent an open alignment with China, and often spoke of evenhandedness. Brzezinski, on the other hand, favored a tilt toward China in a Sino-American-Japanese entente directed against the Soviet Union.

In August 1979, Vice-President Walter Mondale went to China for a week's visit. In a speech at Peking University on August 27, he stated, "Any nation which seeks to weaken or isolate you in world affairs assumes a stance counter to American interests. This is why the United States normalized relations with your country, and that is why we must work to broaden and strengthen our new friendship. . . . Today the unprecedented and friendly relations among China, Japan, and the United States bring international stability to northeast Asia."

China was now clearly emerging in American policy as a bulwark against the Soviet Union. In October 1979, it was revealed that a secret Pentagon study recommended U.S. arms sales to the People's Republic. Secretary Vance strongly denied that the United States had any intention of changing its arms policy on China.

But the Soviet invasion of Afghanistan in December 1979 underlined the U.S. need of China as an Asian ally. The visit to China of U.S. Defense Secretary Harold Brown, in January 1980, which had been scheduled before the Soviet invasion, gave the United States for the first time a closeup look at Chinese defenses. Brown reiterated Vance's denials, but discussed Sino-American cooperation in strengthening Pakistan's defense. He also called for "parallel actions" by the United States and China to meet the Russian entry into Afghanistan, and indicated that the United States would consider increased sale to China of high-technology products. Though actual sales of arms continued to be ruled out, exchange visits of military personnel were suggested.

On January 29, 1980, a British newspaper carried a report

that Soviet President Brezhnev warned that the nuclear arming of the Chinese would lead to Soviet preemptive strikes on China.

To bring Sino-American relations full circle, the U.S. Congress, in January 1980, granted China most-favored-nation status for trade purposes. Carter had agreed to this important concession the year before, intending to extend it to the Soviet Union at the same time, but the Soviet invasion of Afghanistan made that impossible. The U.S.–Soviet SALT II agreement was also tabled for the time being, and the American-Chinese relationship at last seemed stronger than that of the United States with the Soviet Union. China was finally accepted as an equal among nations.

LOOKING TO
THE FUTURE

The rapid change in American-Chinese relations has baffled even the most knowledgeable experts. Any predictions concerning the future must be speculative and unreliable. As some questions about the future are answered, others will arise. Yet it is possible to point to possible directions, given current trends.

The three main questions for the future of the Sino-American relationship are the following:

1. What is the likely course of the People's Republic of China and what will it mean for the United States?
2. How will the two-China problem be resolved?
3. What role is the United States to play in relation to China and the Soviet Union?

In China itself, its aging leadership seeks to proceed as rapidly as possible with the "four modernizations"—in agriculture, industry, science and technology, and defense. To accomplish these aims, China needs assistance from the outside, and the United States offers the main source of that help. As long as the aim of the Chinese government is modernization, it is likely to maintain ties to the West. Thus whether the leadership under Deng Xiaoping succeeds in making the modernization program irreversible will strongly influence the future of U.S.–China relations.

Deng sought to rebuild the middle-level Chinese leadership and place in positions of authority those sympathetic to modernization. Early in 1980, Deng began to relinquish some of his posts, allowing younger men to rise to leadership. In September, Hua Guofeng was replaced as prime minister by Zhao Ziyang, although Hua retained his post as party chairman. Zhao, the former Communist Party chief of Sichuan province, was backed by Deng for the leadership role. Rather than indicating a change of policy, these moves seem to indicate an effort to move the power from the present generation of leaders to the next in orderly fashion.

Deng was quoted in a Bangkok newspaper in February 1980 on the problems of succession: "People of my age should really be concerned about arranging for what comes after. By that I mean we must find good and reliable successors so that once the succession takes place, new turmoil will not break out again."

Deng also sought to remove the Maoist hard-liners from authority so that China would not be able to revert once again to a self-destructive period of ideological purity.

For a time China's new rulers allowed criticism from its citizens, expressed in the form of "wall posters." Western diplomats viewed the public display of these posters with amazement, for they compared Chinese society unfavorably to that of the United States and even to Taiwan. It was clear that the Chinese leadership wanted a safety valve for the smoldering questions that had arisen during the long period when Mao's teachings were the absolute policy throughout China. But on December 6, 1979, the "Democracy wall" in Peking was closed.

Pressures within China remain. Seymour Topping, managing editor of *The New York Times,* reported after a trip to China in early 1980 that the effects of the Cultural Revolution are still being felt in Shanghai, with "thousands of desperate, rootless young people in the city. They have broken into public buildings, blocked street traffic, contributed to an upsurge of crime." According to Topping, 17 million students were "shipped out of China's cities into rural areas" during the Cultural Revolution, and "Since 1976, millions have wandered back to their home cities, demanding permission to stay, demanding jobs."

In a speech in Janury 1980, Deng listed China's three major tasks of the 1980s: (1) economic modernization, (2) the reunification of Taiwan, and (3) combating the Soviet Union. Of the three, said the vice-premier, "Everything depends on the speed and size of our economic development."

Though China's most-favored-nation status will help in establishing trade, China must develop trade credits by selling abroad its own products and resources. One of the more promising areas of Chinese exports is likely to be oil. Offshore in the China Sea, there are already nineteen U.S. oil companies and fifteen other foreign oil interests doing exploratory surveys. The Chinese are interested in letting foreign companies develop inland resources as well.

Acceptance of Western technology also depends on China's ability to use it. At the individual level, China is still a poor country where it is more economical to use hand labor than to mechanize the means of production.

THE TWO-CHINA PROBLEM

The contrasting prosperity of Taiwan is one of the obstacles to the unification of the "two Chinas." Economically Taiwan is one of the most prosperous countries in Asia. In 1979 its trade with the United States was approximately $9.5 billion, an increase of more than $2 billion over the last year of full diplomatic relations.

Some of the fears and warnings of those Americans who opposed severing ties with Taiwan have proved groundless. The United States has continued much the same trade and cultural relationship. Arms deals after the one-year moratorium that ended January 1980 are considered likely.

Though fewer nations recognize Taiwan officially, its overall trade was up more than 30 percent in 1979 over the preceding year.

Taiwan has not developed an atomic bomb to defend itself, nor has it publicly turned toward the Soviet Union, though rumors of diplomatic feelers have been published. Taiwan, during 1979, did begin to cultivate markets in Communist Eastern Europe, permitting direct trade for the first time with Poland, Yugoslavia, Hungary, East Germany, and Czechoslovakia. This direct contact with Communist nations was regarded as a hopeful sign for eventual reconciliation with the People's Republic.

Despite its prosperity, Taiwan must deal with the problem of domestic dissent. On December 10, 1979, demonstrators in Kaohsiung clashed with riot police. In March 1980, staff members of a magazine called *Formosa* were tried on charges connected with the riot. A crackdown on dissidents followed. According to government claims, *Formosa* magazine was established in August 1979 as part of an opposition movement aimed at the overthrow of the government. There is some sentiment both within Taiwan and outside for abandonment of the claims to sovereignty over all of China and a declaration of the independence of Taiwan as a separate nation. Overseas, a New York–based organization called United Formosans for Independence supports this movement.

While Chiang's son rules, there is little possiblity that Taiwan will abandon its claims to China. In Taiwan, fraternization with citizens of the mainland and contact with outsiders calling for Taiwanese independence are seditious offenses. The independence movement remains small, and the Nationalists (15 percent of the total population of Taiwan) who are non-Taiwanese and have ruled since 1949, show no signs of relinquishing their control of the island.

A hopeful sign for the future is the increase in links between Taiwan and the People's Republic since the United States switched its recognition policy. Shipments from Taiwan to China through the British territory of Hong Kong increased from $50,000 in the first six months of 1978 to $3 million in the comparable period of 1979. Also in 1979 Taiwan abandoned its policy of boycotting international meetings where the People's Republic was represented. There were at least eighteen meetings in 1979 at which both the People's Republic and Taiwan were represented.

There were other signs that the tension between the two Chinas was lessening. As of January 1, 1979, Taiwan and the People's Republic ceased their practice of shelling each other from the mainland and the Nationalist-held offshore islands. Goods from the mainland have been allowed entry into Taiwan. Taiwanese newspapers have increased their coverage of developments within mainland China, including some favorable commentary on mainland Chinese students who were befriended by Taiwanese students in the United States—something hitherto strictly forbidden.

THE EFFECT ON
U.S.–SOVIET RELATIONS

The most pressing question for the United States remains: What effect will its new policy toward China have on the U.S. relationship with the Soviet Union?

It seems clear that the sheer fact of rapprochement with the most populous nation in the world strengthens the American position in strategic terms. The *Washington Post,* in an editorial of January 11, 1980, said, "The fact of the China connection is for Washington its greatest strategic benefit: just by existing, the connection halves the number of our nuclear-armed foes."

The first year of normalization witnessed a steady growth of Sino-American relations. According to the People's Republic, 308 official delegations came to the United States in 1979; about 40,000 U.S. tourists and an uncounted number of American delegations visited China in the first year of normalization. At the end of January 1980, a delegation of scientists headed by White House science adviser Frank Press went to China to discuss the area of cooperation most important to Peking—Sino-American scientific and technical cooperation.

American use of China to influence the triangular relationship with the USSR has been termed "playing the China card." In global terms, the USSR has taken note of the "China card" as a threat important enough to warn the United States against playing it. But the Carter administration, while denying it, has indeed attempted to use the China card as a block to Soviet expansionism, for instance in the Afghanistan crisis.

However, the Carter administration displayed an inconsistency of views regarding the China card. On December 20, 1979, Secretary of Defense Harold Brown told the Senate Foreign Relations Committee in secret session that "It is important that we not feed Soviet paranoia by appearing to tilt toward the PRC."

Yet before long President Carter postponed indefinitely Senate consideration of the ratification of the SALT II disarmament treaty. Moreover, the USSR was left out of the plan to extend most-favored-nation trade status to both the Communist superpowers, and the concession was granted only to the Chinese.

The White House, in the aftermath of Soviet aggression in Afghanistan, continued to put out the impression that the American response was not merely to put SALT II on ice, but also to punish the Russians by establishing a military relationship with the Chinese.

Certainly, Secretary Brown's statements during his visit to China in January 1980 left the impression that the United States was going to build up Chinese military forces. Brown discussed not merely general ties with the Chinese, but specific military moves, including American overflights of China to supply Afghanistan's neighbor, Pakistan, with military aid.

The Chinese did not give a clear yes or no to the Brown proposals. The Chinese seemed less willing to play the "American card." One American official commented, "China does not like to be used tactically." An American delegation to China was told by a professor at the Chinese Academy of Social Sciences, "You Americans are so charming, you have such short memories. We can't forget so fast or so easily what happened between us in the past."

Nor was American support for playing the China card unanimous. *The New York Times,* in an editorial in February 1980, commented, "Within the lifetime of any American over 60, China has been perceived successively as a worthy missionary cause, a valiant wartime ally, the most implacable of enemies, and finally a strange new friend, even a potential brother-in-arms. In plain fact, China is now a totalitarian society, ruled by aging sectarians who one day allow a 'democracy wall' only to reverse themselves when speech becomes too free. The country is poor, its weapons largely obsolete. The Pentagon thinks it would cost up to $60 billion to equip China to defend itself against even a nonnuclear Soviet attack."

Carter himself told visiting congresspersons on January 8, 1980, "We are not going to play the China card against the Soviet Union . . . but I think it's appropriate to improve our relations with China."

The immediate course for U.S. policy toward China is disputed between those who favor evenhandedness and those who advocate a full tilt toward China—laying the China card on the table to await a Soviet response.

For those favoring evenhandedness, the argument is that by siding with neither the USSR nor the People's Republic, but playing them off against one another, the United States has more to gain than by favoring one or the other. Those arguing this position maintain that world stability depends on the U.S.'s remaining neutral in the Sino-Soviet split.

Too close a relationship with the People's Republic could drop the United States into China's quarrels in Asia, for instance in Vietnam. If American policy were seen to favor Peking, the Soviet Union might react in unforeseen ways that might not be to the West's advantage. One reason for the massive Soviet arms buildup of the 1970s and 1980s has been the tension between it and its immense neighbor to the south. The Soviet Union has given clear signals that it will not tolerate American nuclear aid to China. How much aid they will tolerate remains an unknown.

On the other hand, if the Chinese perceived the Americans as favoring the Russians, they could turn back to some kind of alliance with the Soviet Union, dangerously altering the balance of power against the West.

Opposing the arguments for evenhandedness are those American policy-planners who view the Soviet Union as the U.S.'s main adversary. By their argument, the United States should treat the Chinese as friends despite the differing ideologies and provide the Chinese with American expertise extending even to the military sphere. Those favoring this position point out that China poses no military threat to the United States, and say China should be rewarded for its independence from Moscow. They argue that failure to reward the Chinese for independence might lead to a new pro-Soviet leadership in Peking.

Events have shown that American policy will have to be based not entirely on Washington's calculations, but on worldwide events. A Rand Corporation (policy study think-tank) report issued December 28, 1979, said, "Should the Soviet Union continue its efforts to encircle China with political allies and military bases, countries such as Japan, the United States, and the states of Western Europe will come under greater pressure to ally themselves with the People's Republic of China to counter Moscow's increasingly assertive foreign policy."

In China itself, the future is far from clear. Deng's efforts to secure a smooth transition of power, if successful, may well produce a generation of younger leaders dedicated to his plans for modernization and accommodation with the West. But a take-over by hard-line leaders nurtured in the fires of Mao's Cultural Revolution could throw all American policy calculations out the window.

Similarly Taiwan itself could be the source of future developments affecting the Sino-American relationship. Should a Taiwanese government declare independence as a separate nation, the United States would be hard pressed to keep its agreement with Peking that Taiwan is part of China. Deng has thus far shown no inclination to try to take Taiwan by force. One future for Taiwan might be peaceful incorporation into China as a semiautonomous province. China and Taiwan retain the strong ties of language and culture. But other leaders than Deng might prove less patient.

There are hopeful signs. The USSR showed remarkable restraint when it held back a military response to China's invasion of Vietnam. China itself stirs with voices that question the policies of the past and seek knowledge and contact with an America that till recently was a mortal enemy. Finally, the United States has progressed a long way in understanding China from the time when China was regarded as its to "lose." China still remains a mystery to Americans, but one that we approach from the standpoint of equality and a need for greater understanding.

FOR FURTHER READING

Bailey, Thomas A. *A Diplomatic History of the American People.* 10th ed. Englewood Cliffs, N.J.: Prentice-Hall, 1980.

Committee of Concerned Asian Scholars. *China! Inside the People's Republic.* New York: Bantam Books, 1972.

Congressional Quarterly eds. *China–U.S. Policy Since 1945.* Washington, D.C.: Congressional Quarterly, 1980.

Davies, John Paton, Jr. *Dragon by the Tail.* New York: W. W. Norton, 1972.

Fairbank, John King. *The United States and China.* 4th ed. Cambridge, Mass.: Harvard University Press, 1979.

Greene, Fred. *The Far East.* New York: Holt, Rinehart & Winston, 1962.

Kahn, E. J., Jr. *The China Hands.* New York: Penguin Books, 1975.

Milton, David; Milton, Nancy; and Schurmann, Franz, eds. *People's China: Social Experimentation, Politics, Entry onto the World Scene, 1966 through 1972.* New York: Random House, Vintage Books, 1974.

Schaller, Michael. *The United States and China in the Twentieth Century.* New York: Oxford University Press, 1979.

Schurmann, Franz, and Schell, Orville, eds. *Communist China: Revolutionary Reconstruction and International Confrontation, 1949 to the Present.* New York: Random House, Vintage Books, 1967.

————*Republican China: Nationalism, War, and the Rise of Communism, 1911–1949.* New York: Random House, Vintage Books, 1967.

Snow, Edgar. *Red China Today.* New York: Random House, Vintage Books, 1971.

Terrill, Ross. *The Future of China.* New York: Dell, Delta Books, 1978.

————*800,000,000: The Real China.* New York: Dell, 1972.

Tuchman, Barbara W. *Stilwell and the American Experience in China, 1911–45.* New York: Macmillan, 1971.

Yim, Kwan Ha, ed. *China and the U.S., 1955–63.* New York: Facts on File, 1973.

————*China and the U.S., 1964–72.* New York: Facts on File, 1975.

INDEX